Morphology of the Folktale

American Folklore Society Bibliographical and Special Series
Volume 9/Revised Edition/1968

Indiana University Research Center in Anthropology, Folklore, and Linguistics
Publication 10/Revised Edition/1968

Morphology of the Folktale

by

V. Propp

First Edition Translated by Laurence Scott with an Introduction by Svatava Pirkova–Jakobson

Second Edition Revised and Edited with a Preface by Louis A. Wagner/New Introduction by Alan Dundes

University of Texas Press

International Standard Book Number 0-292-78376-0 (paper)

Library of Congress Catalog Card Number 68-65567

Printed in the United States of America

Eighth Paperback Printing, 1984

CONTENTS

PREFACE TO THE SECOND EDITION

THE PREPARATION of this second English edition of Vladímir Propp's *Morphology of the Folktale* had two major objectives. The first was to make some changes in the text of the first edition for the sake of completeness and uniformity. In this regard, note should be taken of one general convention adopted for the present edition: the expression *naródnaja skázka* has been rendered as "folktale," *volšébnaja skázka* as "fairy tale," and the words *skázka* (noun), *skázočnyj* (adjective) simply as "tale." The chief departure from this practice is in regard to the title itself (*Morfológija skázki*), since a change here might have led to undue confusion. The morphology presented by the author is, of course, a morphology of the fairy tale specifically, and he is careful to make note of this fact in the Foreword and in Chapter II. Thus the title of the work is, unfortunately, somewhat unclear. It is evident from the text that the unqualified word *skázka* is used by Propp both in the sense of tale in general and in the sense of fairy tale, depending upon context. The reader must infer the appropriate meaning in each instance.

The second major objective was to update the author's numerical references to tales contained in the collection *Naródnye rússkie skázki* by A. N. Afanás'ev, so that they would correspond to the sequential enumeration of texts which was adopted for the fifth (1936–1940) and sixth (1957) editions of that fundamental work. Propp's basic corpus of material, tales numbered 50 to 151 in the earlier editions (with letters designating similar texts, e.g. 140a, b, c, etc.) and cited by him, are consequently numbered 93 to 270 in the last two editions of Afanás'ev and in the present works. A list of pertinent correspondences between the newer and older numbers is provided in Appendix V.

The updating of the numerical references, however, required that many of them be checked against the tales themselves, as the original text of *Morfológija skázki* contains a number of obvious misprints and other inconsistencies, especially in regard to the citation of these references and to the use of symbols in the schemes and elsewhere. Therefore, in an attempt to make the present edition as useful as possible, a systematic check of all textual references relating to the tales themselves was undertaken, and those numbers found to be in error were corrected. Every instance of correction is described in a footnote.

The checking of references incidentally revealed other inconsistencies or, at any rate, instances of careless phrasing in the utilization of these references by the author. However, no attempt at emendation was made in such cases; rather, they also are described in footnotes, generally accompanied by inclusion of the original text. It should be noted that the checking of references did not include those made by the author in his own footnotes—they are reproduced essentially as presented.

The few minor changes which were felt necessary, apart from those described, are appropriately indicated. One feature of the original work has not been preserved: a number of chapters are headed by quotations from Goethe, and these have been dropped as nonessential.

I wish to thank Frank Ingram and Stephen Soudakoff of Indiana University for their careful comparison of the original text with my revised translation, which resulted in many emendations and helpful suggestions.

Indiana University
1968

LOUIS A. WAGNER

INTRODUCTION TO THE SECOND EDITION

Since the appearance of the English translation of Vladímir Propp's *Morphology of the Folktale* in 1958, there has been an ever increasing interest in attempting structural analyses of various folklore genres. In view of the enormous impact Propp's study has had on folklorists, linguists, anthropologists, and literary critics, one can only regret that there was a thirty-year time lag between Propp's completion of the *Morphology* in 1928 and the time that most European and American scholars read it.

The stimulating effect of Propp's seminal ideas is indicated in part by the number of studies it has inspired (Lévi-Strauss 1960, Dundes 1962a, 1964b, Bremond 1964, Greimas 1966b:172–221). To be sure, some of the studies are critical (cf. Taylor 1964), but from the criticism has come even more insight (e.g., Fischer 1963:288–289). Even though the flurry of activity initiated by the publication of Propp's *Morphology* has really barely begun, some preliminary comments may be made.

First of all, there seem to be at least two distinct types of structural analysis in folklore. One is the type of which Propp's *Morphology* is the exemplar par excellence. In this type, the structure or formal organization of a folkloristic text is described following the chronological order of the linear sequence of elements in the text as reported from an informant. Thus if a tale consists of elements A to Z, the structure of the tale is delineated in terms of this same sequence. Following Lévi-Strauss (1964: 312), this linear sequential structural analysis we might term "syntagmatic" structural analysis, borrowing from the notion of syntax in the study of language (cf. Greimas 1966a:404). The other type of structural analysis in folklore seeks to describe the pattern (usually based upon an a priori binary principle of opposition) which allegedly underlies the folkloristic text. This pattern is not the same as the sequential structure at all. Rather the elements are taken out of the "given" order and are regrouped in one or more analytic schema. Patterns or organization in this second type of structural analysis might be termed "paradigmatic" (cf. Sebag 1963:75), borrowing from the notion of paradigms in the study of language.

The champion of paradigmatic structural analysis is Claude Lévi-Strauss and it should be noted that he presented a paradigmatic model as early as 1955, that is, well before the English translation of Propp's work. The hypothetical paradigmatic matrix is typically one in which polar oppositions such as life/death, male/female are mediated. Lévi-Strauss is certainly aware of the distinction between Propp's syntagmatic structure and his paradigmatic structure. In fact, Lévi-Strauss's position is essentially that linear sequential structure is but apparent or manifest content, whereas the paradigmatic or schematic structure is the more important latent content. Thus the task of the structural analyst, according to Lévi-Strauss, is to see past or through the superficial linear structure to the "correct" or true underlying paradigmatic pattern of organization (Lévi-Strauss 1955: 432; 1958:18; 1964:313). Although some of the differences between syntagmatic and paradigmatic analyses have been pointed out (cf. Waugh 1966:161), most folklorists are not aware of them and they wrongly lump both Propp and Lévi-Strauss together in the same category. (Propp himself attempted to comment on Lévi-Strauss's extended critique of the *Morphology* but this exchange is available only in the 1966 Italian translation of Propp's work to which Lévi-Strauss's 1960 critique and Propp's rejoinder are appended.) Generally speaking, the syntagmatic approach tends to be both empirical and inductive, and its resultant analyses can be replicated. In contrast, paradigmatic analyses are speculative and deductive, and they are not as easily replicated. (For examples of paradigmatic analyses, see the studies by Greimas, Leach, Sebag, and Köngäs and Maranda.)

One of the most important differences in emphasis between the syntagmatic and paradigmatic brands of structural analysis has been the concern or lack of concern with context. Propp's syntagmatic approach has unfortunately dealt with the structure of text alone, just as literary folklorists generally have considered the text in isolation from its social and cultural context (cf. Dundes 1964c). In this sense, pure formalistic structural analysis is probably every bit as sterile as motif-hunting and word-counting. In contrast, Lévi-Strauss has bravely attempted to relate the paradigm(s) he "finds" in myth to the world at large, that is, to other aspects of culture such as cosmology and world view. It is in this light that Lévi-Strauss's approach has helped lead to the new notion of myth (and other forms of folklore) as *models*. (Note that Malinowski's basically diachronic conception of myth as charter [set back in primeval time] has had to be updated to include a more synchronic conception of myth as model. The intellectual shift from "myth as charter" to "myth as model" is surely one significant consequence of synchronic structural analysis.) However, the emphasis upon context is rather one of application of the results of structural analysis than one inherent in the paradigmatic approach. The problem is that Propp made no attempt to relate his extraordinary morphology to Russian (or Indo-European) culture as a whole. Clearly, structural analysis is not an end in itself! Rather it is a beginning, not an end. It is a powerful technique of descriptive ethnography inasmuch as it lays bare the essential form of the folkloristic text. But the form must ultimately be related to the culture or cultures in which it is found. In this sense, Propp's study is only a first step, albeit a giant one. For example, does not the fact that Propp's last function is a wedding indicate that Russian fairy-tale structure has something to do with marriage? Is the fairy tale a model, a model of fantasy to be sure, in which one begins with an old nuclear family (cf. Propp's typical initial situation "The members of a family are enumerated" or Function 1, "One of the members of a family is absent from home") and ends finally with the formation of a new family (Function 31, "The hero is married and ascends the throne")? Whether this is so or not, there is certainly no reason in theory why the syntagmatic structure of folktales cannot be meaningfully related to other aspects of a culture (such as social structure).

Many other fruitful areas of investigation are opened up by Propp's study. To what extent is Propp's *Morphology* an analysis of *Russian* fairy tales (as opposed to the fairy tales of other cultures)? Many, if not all, of the tales are Aarne-Thompson tale types and thus Propp's analysis is clearly not limited to Russian materials. On the other hand, Propp's *Morphology* provides a useful point of departure for studies attempting to identify oicotypes. Von Sydow's notion of oicotype (1948:243) meaning a recurrent, predictable cultural or local variant must be amended in view of Propp's work to include oicotypes of structure as well as of content. Thus in addition to local penchants for specific content (motifs) within stable cross-cultural frames (such as Aarne-Thompson tale types), there may be culturally favored structural patterns (motifemic sequences) as well (cf. Dundes 1962b, 1964b:99–100).

Some of the other questions arising from Propp's work include: to what extent is Propp's analysis applicable to forms of the folktale other than the fairy tale? The English title *Morphology of the Folktale* is misleading. Propp limits his analysis to only one kind of folktale, that is, to fairy tales or Aarne-Thompson tale types 300–749. What about the other Aarne-Thompson folktale types? If, for example, Von Sydow is correct in grouping Aarne-Thompson tale types 850–879 under what he calls *chimerates* (the major portion of which are Aarne-Thompson types 300–749), then presumably Propp's analysis should also apply to this group of tales (cf. Von Sydow 1948:70). There is also the question of whether Propp's analysis might be applicable to non-Indo-European folktales. Attempts to study African tales (Paulme) and American Indian tales (Dundes 1964b) suggest that parts of Propp's *Morphology* may be cross-culturally valid.

Another question concerns the extent to which Propp's analysis applies to forms of folk narrative other than the folktale. For example, what is the relationship of Propp's *Morphology* to the structure of epic? (In this connection, it is noteworthy that the last portion of the *Odyssey* is strikingly similar to Propp's functions 23–31.) To what extent does Propp's analysis apply to genres of folklore other than those of folk narrative? It would appear that the structure of folk dances and games may be illuminated by Propp's analysis (Dundes 1964a). And what of the structure of nonfolkloristic materials? If there is a pattern in a culture, it is by no means necessary that it be limited to only one aspect of that culture. Quite the contrary. Culture patterns normally manifest themselves in a variety of cultural materials. Propp's analysis should be useful in analyzing the structure of literary forms (such as novels and plays), comic strips, motion-picture and television plots, and the like. In understanding the interrelationship between folklore and literature, and between folklore and the mass media, the emphasis has hitherto been principally upon content. Propp's *Morphology* suggests that there can be structural borrowings as well as content borrowings.

Propp's *Morphology* may also have important implications for studies of thinking and learning processes. To what extent is the structure of the fairy tale related to the structure of the ideal success story in a culture? (This also asks whether actual behavior is critically influenced by the type of fairy-tale structure found in a given culture.) And how precisely is fairy-tale structure learned? Does the child unconsciously extrapolate fairy-tale structure from hearing many individual fairy tales? Do children become familiar enough with the general nature of fairy-tale morphology to object to or question a deviation from it by a storyteller? (This kind of question may be investigated by field and laboratory experiments. For example, part of an actual or fictitious (=nontraditional) fairy tale containing the first several functions of Propp's analysis could be presented to a child who would be asked to "finish" the story. His completion could be checked against the rest of Propp's functions. Or a tale could be told with a section left out, e.g., the donor sequence, functions 12–14, and the child asked to fill in the missing portion. Such tests might also be of value in studies of child psychology. Presumably, the kinds of choices made by a child might be related to his personality. For example, does a little boy select a female donor figure to aid him against a male villain? Does a little girl select a male donor figure to assist her against her wicked stepmother?) In any case, while there have been many studies of language learning, there have been very few dealing with the acquisition of folklore. Certainly children "learn" riddle structure almost as soon as they learn specific riddles. Propp's *Morphology* thus provides an invaluable tool for the investigation of the acquisition of folklore.

Finally, Propp's scheme could also be used to generate new tales. In fact, Propp's *Morphology* has been programmed for a computer (Dundes 1965). Such techniques might be of interest to those seeking new species of literature based on folk form and content, or to those seeking to show the traditional nature and limited number of the combinations of narrative motifs actually found in oral tradition as opposed to the total number of theoretically possible combinations. In addition, analysis of the "rules" by which tales or portions (Propp's *moves*) of tales are generated or transformed is clearly another research prospect made possible by Propp's pioneering study.

There can be no doubt that Propp's analysis is a landmark in the study of folklore. Despite the fact that there is no mention of it in the standard treatises on the folktale, Propp's *Morphology* will in all probability be regarded by future generations as one of the major theoretical breakthroughs in the field of folklore in the twentieth century.

REFERENCES

Bremond, Claude

1964 Le message narratif. *Communications* 4:4–32.

1966 La logique des possibles narratifs. *Communications* 8:60–76.

Buchler, Ira R., and Henry A. Selby

1968 *A Formal Study of Myth,* Center for Intercultural Studies in Folklore and Oral History Monograph Series No. 1. Austin, Texas.

Dundes, Alan

1962a From Etic to Emic Units in the Structural Study of Folktales. *Journal of American Folklore* 75:95–105.

1962b The Binary Structure of 'Unsuccessful Repetition' in Lithuanian Folk Tales. *Western Folklore* 21:165–174.

1964a On Game Morphology: A Study of the Structure of Non-Verbal Folklore. *New York Folklore Quarterly* 20:276–288.

1964b *The Morphology of North American Indian Folktales,* FFC 195. Helsinki.

1964c Texture, Text, and Context. *Southern Folklore Quarterly* 28:251–265.

1965 On Computers and Folktales. *Western Folklore* 24:185–189.

Fischer, J. L.

1963 The Sociopsychological Analysis of Folktales. *Current Anthropology* 4: 235–295.

Greimas, A. J.

1963 La Description de la Signification et la Mythologie Comparée. *L'Homme* 3, no. 3:51–66.

1965 Le conte populaire Russe (Analyse fonctionnelle). *International Journal of Slavic Linguistics and Poetics* 9:152–175.

1966a Elementi per una teoria dell'interpretazione del racconto mitico. *Rassegna Italiana Di Sociologia* 7:389–438.

1966b *Sémantique structurale.* Paris.

1966c Structure et Histoire. *In Problèmes du Structuralisme* (special issue) *Les Temps Modernes* 22:815–827.

Köngäs [Maranda], Elli Kaija, and Pierre Maranda

1962 Structural Models in Folklore. *Midwest Folklore* 12:133–192.

Leach, Edmund

1961 Lévi-Strauss in the Garden of Eden: An Examination of Some Recent Developments in the Analysis of Myth. *Transactions of the New York Academy of Sciences,* Ser. II, 23:386–396.

1967 *The Structural Study of Myth and Totemism*. Association of Social Anthropologists Monographs No. 5. London and New York.

Lévi-Strauss, Claude
1955 The Structural Study of Myth. *Journal of American Folklore* 68:428–444.
1958 La Geste D'Asdiwal. *In l'Annuaire 1958–59, Ecole pratique des Hautes Études (Section des Sciences religieuses)*. Paris. Pp. 2–43. (English translation in Leach 1967:1–47)
1960 L'analyse morphologique des contes russes. *International Journal of Slavic Linguistics and Poetics* 3:122–149.
1964 *Mythologiques: Le Cru et Le Cuit*. Paris.
1966 *Mythologiques: Du Miel aux Cendres*. Paris.

Levin, Isidor
1967 Vladimir Propp: An Evaluation on His Seventieth Birthday. *Journal of the Folklore Institute* 4:32–49.

Paci, Enzo
1965 Il senso delle strutture in Lévi-Strauss. *Revue Internationale de Philosophie* 73–74:300–313.

Paulme, Denise
1963 Le garçon travesti ou Joseph en Afrique. *L'Homme* 3, no. 2:5–21.

Pop, Mihai
1967 Aspects actuels des recherches sur la structure des contes. *Fabula* 9:70–77.

Pouillon, Jean
1966 L'Analyse des Mythes. *L'Homme,* 6, no. 1:100–105.

Propp, Vladímir
1966 *Morfologia Della Fiaba*. Torino.

Rohan-Csermak, Géza de
1965 Structuralisme et folklore. *In IVth International Congress for Folk-Narrative Research*. Athens. Pp. 399–407.

Sebag, Lucien
1963 La Geste de Kasewat. *L'Homme,* 3, no. 2:22–76.
1965 Le Mythe: Code et Message. *Les Temps Modernes* 20:1607–1623.

Taylor, Archer
1964 The Biographical Pattern in Traditional Narrative. *Journal of the Folklore Institute,* 1:114–129.

Thion, Serge
1966 Structurologie. *In Le Structuralisme* (special issue), Aletheia 4:219–227.

Von Sydow, C. W.
1948 *Selected Papers on Folklore,* Laurits Bødker, ed. Copenhagen.

Waugh, Butler
1966 Structural Analysis in Literature and Folklore. *Western Folklore* 25:153–164.

University of California
Berkeley, California
February, 1968

ALAN DUNDES

INTRODUCTION TO THE FIRST EDITION

THE SUBJECT OF THIS STUDY, the Russian fairy tale (*volšébnaja skázka*), is the most numerous and artistically the most elaborate of the Slavic folktales. Also, as Jiří Polívka, the great Czech folklorist, demonstrates in his comparative studies of the Slavic folktale, its structural and formal complexity has no equivalent in the fairy tales either of Western Europe or of the Eastern, non-Slavic neighbors of Russia. Nonetheless, it is just the archaic features of the Russian fairy tale that are its exclusive national trademark. There are a few historical, cultural, and social factors that lie in the background of this striking folklore phenomenon. To begin with, the verbal art of all the Eastern and Southern Slavic territory, in general, has always been of preponderantly epic character, so that, in contrast to the Slavic West, the narrative genres both in prose and verse were particularly strongly developed in Russian, Bulgarian, and Serbian folklore. Furthermore, since in Russia written literature was, until the seventeenth century, used only for religious themes, ecclesiastic purposes, and the Church Slavonic language, the Russian fairy tale, specifically, could evolve without any literary influence from above. The custom of tale-telling having been practiced among all the social classes, the artistic tools of the narrator became progressively sharpened; the demands of the listener became more and more refined; and the narrative codes of the fairy tale were step by step crystallized under the influence of this social censorship. The art of narration and dramatic presentation, together with a keen sense of the oral epic style, became a characteristic quality of the Russian people.

No wonder then the Russian folktale was reflected in the Russian popular tale of the eighteenth century, left its unmistakable imprint on the sophisticated short story, which was being fashioned at that time in Russia after the Western model, and eventually became the primary source from which the greatest Russian writers of the nineteenth century created the Russian literary language.

Russian folktales were first collected on a wide scale by A. N. Afanás'ev. His *Rússkie naródnye skázki,* published in 1855–1864, still stands as the basic Russian folktale collection. The mid-century marks also the beginning of the scientific interest in the folktale in Russia. The Russian ethnographers adapted the mythological and the diffusionist approach of the Western schools to the study of their native folklore. And an original, pioneering work was done by the sociologically oriented folklorists who, beginning in the 1860's, concentrated on the narrator himself and investigated the impact of his creative abilities and of his geographical and social background on the folktale, particularly on the formation of its variants.

The modern Russian studies of the folktale developed in close relation with the new European trends in ethnographic scholarship. When in the 1920's the emphasis was shifted from speculations about origin to the synchronic aspect of the folktale, it was the Aarne-Thompson Index of folktale types that answered the generally felt need for a scientific classification of the common folktale stock. This gigantic achievement of the Finnish-American school launched a new search for a common denominator in the multiformity of the folktale; it inspired new interpretations of the simultaneous occurrence of similar phenomena, and made possible the stating of further specific problems. In Russia, where the Aarne Index of the folktale types was translated and filled out with Russian material, the West European methodological advances coincided with the scholarly offensive of the young formalist school and facilitated its task. The basic tenet of this school was the structural analysis of the literary work. Folklore, owing to its specific features as a collective product—its recurrent, conventionalized and stylized structural components, its highly pronounced formula characteristics and the semantic significance it ascribes to the sound, and stylistic patterns—became the principal experimental ground of the formalists. Linguists, literary historians, and ethnographers investigated the narrative technique of the folktale and the prosody of epic folk poetry, of folksongs, proverbs and riddles. In fact, the leading formalist theoretician, Víktor Šklóvskij, began his innovatory studies of prose with the Russian fairy tale.

The author of the present volume, Vladímir Propp, was an outstanding member of the Russian formalist group, and his

Morphology of the Folktale presents a brilliant example of the orthodox formalist method, applied to the structural analysis of the fairy tale. Operating with a comparatively limited corpus of fairy tales chosen from the Afanás'ev folktale collection, his aim was a description of the fairy tale per se. In his analysis he departs from the smallest narrative units, the motifs; he defines the motifs in terms of their function, that is, in terms of what the dramatis personae do, independently of by whom and in what way the function is fulfilled. He states the number of these functions obligatory for the fairy tale and classifies them according to their significance and position in the course of the narrative. Their sequence is finally the basis of his typology within the genre. He abstracts the compositional pattern that underlies the structure of the fairy tale as a whole and formulates its compositional laws by way of structural signs.

When the *Morphology of the Folktale* appeared in 1928, the formalist trend was already in a state of crisis in Russia. For this reason it was neither translated outside of Russia, nor were its tenets ever discussed in an international forum. However, it exerted some influence. Thus, for instance, Claude Lévi-Strauss applies and even extends Propp's method in his study of myth and in the interpretation of the meaning of myth from its form and structure.

Almost twenty years later, V. Propp returned once more to the subject of the folktale, but this time from a different point of view. In his *Istoríčeskie kórni volšébnoj skázki* ("The Historical Roots of the Fairy Tale"), he abandons the strict study of form and structure and deals instead with the affinities that exist between the fairy tale and religion (myth and ritual) and social institutions at different levels of their evolution. A more specific folklore phenomenon is treated by him in a study of ritual laughter where he shows that ritual laughter in the folktale for instance, often understood as an expression of a purely secular fun, is, in fact, ritualistically linked with myth and incantational magic.

REFERENCES

Andreev, N. *Ukazatel' skazočnyx sjužetov po sisteme Aarne* (Leningrad, 1929).

Bogatyrev, P. and R. Jakobson. *Slavjanskaja filologija v Rossii za gody vojny i revoljucii* (Berlin, 1923).

Erlich, V. *Russian Formalism* (The Hague, 1955).
Jakobson, R. "Commentary," *Russian Fairy Tales* (New York, 1945).
Lévi-Strauss, C. "Structural Study of Myth," *Journal of American Folklore*, LXVIII (1955), 428–43.
Nikíforov, A. "K voprosu o morfologičeskom izučenii narodnoj skazki," *Sbornik Otd. rus. jaz. i slov. Akademii nauk*, CI (1928).
Polívka, J. "Slovanské pohádky," I, *Práce Slovanskeho* Ustavu, VI (1932).
Propp, V. *Morfologija skazki* (Leningrad, 1928).
———. "Transformacii volšebnyx skazok," *Poètika*, IV (1928).
———. "Volšebnoe derevo na mogile," *Sovetskaja ètnografija*, Nos. 1–2 (1934).
———. "Ritual'nyj smex v fol'klore," *Učenye zapiski Leningradskogo Gos. Universiteta*, No. 46. Ser. filol. nauk, vyp. 3 (1939).
———. Istoričeskie korni volšebnoj skazki (Leningrad, 1946).
———. *Russkij geroičeskij èpos* (Leningrad, 1955).
Shaftýmov, A. *Poètika i genezis bylin* (Saratov, 1924).
Šklóvskij, V. *O teorii prozy* (Moscow, 1925); second edition, 1929.
Thompson, Stith. *The Types of the Folktale: Antti Aarne's Verzeichnis der Märchentypen, Translated and Enlarged, FF Communications*, No. 74 (Helsinki, 1928).
Trubetzkóy, N. "O metrike častuški," *Vërsty*, II (Paris, 1927).

1958 SVATAVA PIRKOVA-JAKOBSON

ACKNOWLEDGEMENTS

TWO GRANTS facilitated the appearance of this volume: the translation was supported by the Committee for the Promotion of Advanced Slavic Cultural Studies; and a publication subsidy was received from the Subcommittee on Grants of the Joint Committee on Slavic Studies. We are grateful for their assistance.

The translator wishes to express his appreciation to Jean Berko for helping him with the final version of this translation.

Shelby W. Thompson, Assistant to the Editor of the American Folklore Society, prepared the manuscript for press.

1958 THOMAS A. SEBEOK

AUTHOR'S FOREWORD

THE WORD "morphology" means the study of forms. In botany, the term "morphology" means the study of the component parts of a plant, of their relationship to each other and to the whole—in other words, the study of a plant's structure.

But what about a "morphology of the folktale"? Scarcely anyone has thought about the possibility of such a concept.

Nevertheless, it is possible to make an examination of the forms of the tale which will be as exact as the morphology of organic formations. If this cannot be affirmed for the tale as a whole, in its full extent, it can be affirmed in any case for the so-called fairy tales, that is, tales in the strictest sense of the word. It is to these tales that this work is devoted.

The present study was the result of much painstaking labor. Such comparisons demand a certain amount of patience on the part of the investigator. I tried, however, to find a form of presentation which, by simplifying and abbreviating wherever possible, would not overly tax the reader's patience.

This work went through three phases. At first, it was a broad investigation, with a large number of tables, charts, and analyses. It proved impossible to publish such a work, if for no other reason than its great bulk. An attempt at abbreviation was undertaken, based upon a minimum of bulk with a maximum of content. But such an abbreviated, compressed presentation would be beyond the capacity of the ordinary reader: it would resemble a grammar or a textbook on harmony. The form of presentation had to be altered. True, there are things which are impossible to present in a "popular" manner. Such things are in this work too. Nevertheless, I feel that in its present form this study is accessible to every fancier of the tale, provided he is willing to follow the writer into the labyrinth of the tale's multiformity, which in the end will become apparent to him as an amazing uniformity.

In the interest of a shorter and more vivid presentation it became necessary to renounce many things which would be relevant for a specialist. In addition to the sections presented here, this work in its initial form included also an investigation into the rich sphere of the attributes of dramatis personae (i.e., characters as such); it treated in detail questions of metamorphosis, i.e., of the transformation of the tale. Large comparative charts were included, of which only headings remain in the appendix. A much stricter methodological outline preceded the whole work. The original intention was to present an investigation not only of the morphological, but also of the *logical* structure peculiar to the tale, which laid the groundwork for the study of the tale as myth. The presentation itself was more detailed. Elements which are simply singled out as such in the present work were subjected to thorough examination and comparison. It is the isolation of these elements which constitutes the axis of the entire work and predetermines the conclusions. The experienced reader will be able to complete the outline himself.

Our scholarly institutions offered me wide support, affording me the possibility of exchanging ideas with more experienced scholars. The Folktale Commission of the State Geographical Society, under the direction of Academician S. F. Ól'denburg; the Research Institute at Leningrad State University (Living Antiquities Section), under the directorship of Professor D. K. Zelénin; and the Folklore Section of the Department of Verbal Arts of the State Institute of the History of the Arts, under the direction of Academician V. N. Peretz, discussed the methods and conclusions of this work in its parts and as a whole. The heads of these institutions, as well as other participants in discussions, contributed very worthwhile suggestions, and I extend to all of them my deepest gratitude.

Professor V. M. Žirmúnskij took an especially friendly interest in me. He read a part of this work in its first draft and made several important suggestions. It was on his initiative that this study was submitted to the Institute of the History of the Arts.

If the study is now appearing in print, it is thanks to the Institute and first of all to the director of the Department of Verbal Arts, Víktor Maksímovič Žirmúnskij. I will take the liberty of expressing my deepest thanks and gratitude to him for his support and assistance.

15 July 1927 V. Propp

Morphology of the Folktale

CHAPTER I

On the History of the Problem

Scholarly literature concerning the tale is not especially rich. Apart from the fact that few works are being published, bibliographical sources present the following picture: mostly texts themselves are published; there are quite a number of works concerning particular problems; there are no general works on the tale. Such works as do exist are of an informational rather than an investigatory nature. Yet it is precisely questions of a general character which, more than all others, awaken interest. Their resolution is the aim of scholarship. Professor M. Speránskij characterizes the existing situation in the following way: "Without dwelling on conclusions already reached, scientific anthropology continues its investigations, considering the material already collected as still insufficient for a generalized doctrine. Science, therefore, once again sets about the task of collecting material and evaluating it in the interests of future generations. But what general conclusions will be made and when they can be made is still unknown."[1]

What is the reason for this helplessness, and why has the study of the tale found itself up a blind alley?

Speránskij places the blame on an insufficiency of material. But ten years have elapsed since the above lines were written. During this period the major three-volume work of Bolte and Polívka, *Anmerkungen zu den Kinder- und Hausmärchen der Brüder Grimm,* has been completed.[2] In this study, each tale is presented with its variants from the entire world. The last volume ends with a bibliography which lists sources, i.e., all collections of tales and other materials which contain tales that are known to the authors. This listing consists of about 1200 titles. It is true that among these materials there are those which are incidental and insignificant. But there are also major collections, such as the *Thousand and One Nights,* or the 400 texts of the Afanás'ev collection. But that is not all. An enormous amount of tale material has not yet been published, and, in part, not even described. It is in private hands or stored in the archives of various institutions. Specialists do have access to some of these collections. The Folktale Commission of the Geographic Society, in its *Research Survey for the Year 1926,* registers 531 tales as being available to its members. The preceding survey cites approximately three times as many examples. Thanks to this, the material of Bolte and Polívka can, in certain instances, be augmented.[3] If this is so, then just how great is the number of tales that we have at our disposal in general? And moreover, how many researchers are there who have fully covered even the printed sources?

It is impossible, under these circumstances, to say that "the material already collected is still insufficient." What matters is not the amount of material, but the methods of investigation. At a time when the physical and mathematical sciences possess well-ordered classification, a unified terminology adopted by special conferences, and a methodology improved upon by the transmission from teachers to students, we have nothing comparable. The diversity and the picturesque multiformity of tale material make a clear, accurate organization and solution of problems possible only with great difficulty. Let us examine the manner in which the study of the tale has been carried out and the difficulties which confront us. The present essay does not have the aim of systematically recounting the history of the study of the tale. It is impossible to do so in a brief, introductory chapter; nor is this necessary, since this history has already been treated more than once.[4] We shall try only to elucidate critically several attempts at the solution of some basic problems in the study of the tale and at the same time introduce them to the reader.

It is scarcely possible to doubt that phenomena and objects around us can be studied from the aspect of their composition and structure, or from the aspect of those processes and changes to which they are subject, or from the aspect of their origins. Nor is it necessary to prove that one can speak about the origin of any phenomenon only after that phenomenon has been described.

Meanwhile the study of the tale has been pursued for the most part only genetically, and, to a great extent, without attempts at preliminary, systematic description. We shall not speak at present about the historical study of the tale, but shall speak only about the description of it, for to discuss genetics, without special elucidation of the problem of description as it is usually treated, is completely useless. Before throwing light upon the question of the tale's origin, one must first answer the question as to what the tale itself represents.

Since the tale is exceptionally diverse, and evidently cannot be studied at once in its full extent, the material must be divided into sections, i.e., it must be classified. Correct classification is one of the first steps in a scientific description. The accuracy of all further study depends upon the accuracy of classification. But although classification serves as the foundation of all investigation, it must itself be the result of certain preliminary study. What we see, however, is precisely the reverse: the majority of researchers *begin* with classification, imposing it upon the material from without and not extracting it from the material itself. As we shall see further, the classifiers also frequently violate the simplest rules of division. Here we find one of the reasons for the "blind alley" of which Speránskij speaks. Let us consider a few examples.

The most common division is a division into tales with fantastic content, tales of everyday life, and animal tales.[5] At first glance everything appears to be correct. But involuntarily the question arises, "Don't tales about animals sometimes contain elements of the fantastic to a very high degree?" And conversely, "Don't animals actually play a large role in fantastic tales?" Is it possible to consider such an indicator as sufficiently precise? Afanás'ev, for instance, places the tale about the fisherman and the fish among animal tales. Is he correct or not? If not, then why not? Later on we shall see that the tale ascribes with great ease identical actions to persons, objects, and animals. This rule is mainly true for so-called fairy tales, but it is also encountered in tales in general. One of the best-known examples in this regard is the tale about the sharing of the harvest ("I, Míša, get the heads of the grain; you get the roots"). In Russia, the one deceived is the bear; in the West, the devil. Consequently, this tale, upon introduction of a Western variant, suddenly drops out of the group of animal tales. Where does it belong? It is obviously not a tale of everyday life either, for where in everyday life does one find a harvest divided in such a way? Yet this is also not a tale with a fantastic content. It does not fit at all within the described classification.

Nevertheless, we shall affirm that the above classification is basically correct. Investigators here have proceeded according to instinct, and their words do not correspond to what they have actually sensed. Scarcely anyone will be mistaken in placing the tale about the firebird and the grey wolf among the animal tales. It is also quite clear to us that even Afanás'ev was wrong concerning the tale about the goldfish. But we see this not because animals do or do not figure in tales, but because fairy tales possess a quite particular structure which is immediately felt and which determines their category, even though we may not be aware of it. Every investigator who purports to be classifying according to the above scheme is, in fact, classifying differently. However, in contradicting himself, he actually proceeds correctly. But if this is so, if in the basis of classification there is subconsciously contained the structure of the tale, still not studied or even delineated, then it is necessary to place the entire classification of tales on a new track. It must be transferred into formal, structural features. And in order to do this, these features must be investigated.

However, we are getting ahead of ourselves. The situation described remains unclarified to the present day. Further attempts have not brought about any essential improvements. In his famous work *The Psychology of Peoples,* Wundt proposes the following division: (1) mythological tale-fables (*Mythologische Fabelmärchen*); (2) pure fairy tales (*Reine Zaubermärchen*); (3) biological tales and fables (*Biologische Märchen und Fabeln*); (4) pure animal fables (*Reine Tierfabeln*); (5) "genealogical" tales (*Abstammungsmärchen*); (6) joke tales and fables (*Scherzmärchen und Scherzfabeln*); (7) moral fables (*Moralische Fabeln*).[6]

This classification is much richer than the one previously quoted, but it, too, provokes objections. The "fable" (a term which one encounters five times in seven classes), is a formal category. The study of the fable is just beginning.[7] It is unclear what Wundt meant by it. Furthermore the term "joke tale" is in general unacceptable, since the same tale might be treated both heroically and comically. Still further, the question is raised as to the difference between a "pure animal fable" and a "moral fable." In what way are the "pure fables" not "moral" and vice versa?

The classifications discussed deal with the distribution of tales into categories. Besides the division into *categories,* there is a division according to *theme.*

If a division into categories is unsuccessful, the division according to theme leads to total chaos. We shall not even speak about the fact that such a complex, indefinite concept as "theme" is either left completely undefined or is defined by every author in his own way. Jumping ahead, we shall say that the division of fairy tales according to themes is, in general, impossible. Like the division into categories, it too must be placed on a new track. Tales possess one special characteristic: components of one tale can, without any alteration whatsoever, be transferred to another. Later on this law of transference will be elucidated in greater detail; meanwhile we can limit ourselves to pointing out that Bába Jagá, for example, might appear in the most diverse tales, in the most varied themes. This trait is a specific characteristic of the tale. At the same time, in spite of this characteristic, a theme is usually defined in the following fashion: a part of a tale is selected (often haphazardly, simply because it is striking), the preposition "about" is added to it, and the definition is established. In this way a tale which includes a fight with a dragon is a tale "about fights with dragons"; a tale in which Koščéj appears is a tale "about Koščéj," and so on, there being no single principle for the selection of decisive elements. If we now recall the law of transference, it is logically inevitable that the result will be confusion, or, more accurately, an overlapping classification. Such a classification always distorts the essence of the material under examination. To this is added an inconsistency in the basic principle of division, i.e., one more elementary rule of logic is violated. This situation has continued to the present day.

We shall illustrate this situation by giving two examples. In

1924 there appeared a book on the tale by Professor Vólkov of Odessa.[8] Vólkov states, from the very first pages of his work, that the fantastic tale comprises fifteen themes. These are as follows: (1) about those unjustly persecuted; (2) about the hero-fool; (3) about three brothers; (4) about dragon fighters; (5) about procuring brides; (6) about a wise maiden; (7) about those who have been placed under a spell or bewitched; (8) about the possessor of a talisman; (9) about the possessor of magic objects; (10) about an unfaithful wife; etc.

How these fifteen themes were arrived at is not indicated. If one looks into the principle of this division, one obtains the following: the first class is determined by the complication (what the complication actually is we shall see later); the second class is determined by the character of the hero; the third, by the number of heroes; the fourth, by one moment in the course of the action, and so forth. Thus, a consistent principle of division is totally lacking. The result is actually chaos. Do not tales exist in which three brothers (third category) procure brides for themselves (fifth category)? Does not the possessor of a talisman, with the aid of this talisman, punish his unfaithful wife? Thus, the given classification is not a scientific classification in the precise sense of the word. It is nothing more than a conventional index, the value of which is extremely dubious. Can such a classification be even remotely compared with a classification of plants or animals which is carried out not at first glance, but after an exact and prolonged preliminary study of the material?

Having broached the question of the classification of themes, we cannot pass over Aarne's index of tales without comment.[9] Aarne is one of the founders of the so-called Finnish school. The works of this school form the peak of studies of the tale in our time. This is not the place to give due evaluation to this movement.[10] I shall only point out the fact that a rather significant number of articles and notes on the variants of individual themes exist in scholarly literature. Such variants are sometimes obtained from the least expected sources. A great number of them have been gradually accumulating, but they have not been worked over systematically. It is chiefly to this that the attention of the new trend is directed. Representatives of this school seek out and compare variants of separate themes according to their world-wide distribution. The material is geo-ethnographically arranged according to a known, previously developed system, and then conclusions are drawn as to the basic structure, dissemination, and origins of the themes. This method, however, also evokes a series of objections. As we shall see later on, themes (especially the themes of fairy tales) are very closely related to each other. In order to determine where one theme and its variants end and another begins, one must first have made a comparative study of the themes of the tales, and have accurately established the principle of the selection of themes and variants. However, nothing of the kind exists. The transference of elements is not taken into account here either. The works of this school proceed from the subconscious premise that each theme is something organically whole, that it can be singled out from a number of other themes and studied independently.

At the same time, the fully objective separation of one theme from another and the selection of variants is by no means a simple task. Themes of the tale are so closely linked to one another, and are so mutually interwoven, that this problem requires special preliminary study before they can be extracted. Without such study the investigator is left to his own taste, since objective extraction is not yet possible.

Let us take one example. Among the variants of the tale "Frau Holle," Bolte and Polívka quote tale No. 102 from Afanás'ev (the well-known tale, "Bába Jagá"). They also include a number of other Russian tales—even those in which the witch is replaced by mice or a dragon. But they do not include the tale "Morózko." Why not? For here we have the same expulsion of the stepdaughter and her return with gifts, the same sending of the real daughter and her punishment. Moreover, both "Morózko" and "Frau Holle" represent the personification of winter, even though in the German tale we have the personification in a female form, and in the Russian one, in a male form. But apparently "Morózko," because of the artistic vividness of the tale, became subjectively fixed as a special type of tale, a special independent theme which can have its own variants. In this way we see that there are no completely objective criteria for the separation of one theme from another. Where one researcher sees a new theme, another will see a variant, and vice versa. I have given a very simple example, but difficulties increase with the extension and augmentation of the material.

Be that as it may, the methods of this school, first of all, needed a list of themes. This was the task undertaken by Aarne. His list entered into international usage and rendered the study of the tale an enormous service. Thanks to Aarne's index, a coding of the tale has been made possible. Aarne calls themes *types,* and each type is numbered. A brief, conventional designation of tales (in this instance: by reference to a number in the index), is very convenient. In particular, the Folktale Commission could not have described its material wtihout this list, since the synopsis of 530 tales would have required much space, and in order to become acquainted with this material it would have been necessary to read through all of the synopses. Now, one need only look at the numbers and everything is clear at first glance.

But along with these commendable features, the index also reveals a number of real insufficiencies. As a classification it is not free of the same mistakes that Vólkov makes. The basic categories are as follows: (1) animal tales, (2) tales proper, (3) anecdotes. We easily recognize the previous devices changed to a new form. (It is a bit strange that animal tales are apparently not recognized as tales proper.) Furthermore, one feels like asking, "Do we have such precise knowledge of the concept of the *anecdote* to permit our employing it with complete confidence?" (Cf., the term "fables" used by Wundt.)

We shall not enter into the details of this classification,[11] but shall consider only the fairy tales, which Aarne places in a subclass. I should note here that the introduction of subclasses is one of the services rendered by Aarne, since until his time there had been no thorough working out of a division into genus, species, and varieties. The fairy tales comprise, according to Aarne, the following categories: (1) a supernatural adversary; (2) a supernatural husband (wife); (3) a supernatural task; (4) a supernatural helper; (5) a magic object; (6) supernatural power or knowledge; (7) other supernatural motifs. Almost the same objections pertaining to Vólkov's classification can be repeated here. What, for instance, of those tales in which a *supernatural task* is resolved by a *supernatural helper* (which occurs very often), or those in which a *supernatural spouse* is also a *supernatural helper?*

True, Aarne does not really attempt to establish a scientific classification. His index is important as a *practical reference* and, as such, it has a tremendous significance. But Aarne's index is dangerous for another reason. It suggests notions which are essentially incorrect. Clear-cut division into types does not actually exist; very often it is a fiction. If types do exist, they exist not on the level indicated by Aarne, but on the level of the structural features of similar tales, about which we shall speak later. The proximity of plots, one to another, and the impossibility of a completely objective delimitation leads to the fact that, when assigning a text to one or another type, one often does not know what number to choose. The correspondence between a type and a designated text is often quite approximate. Of the 125 tales listed in the collection of A. I. Nikíforov, 25 tales (i.e., twenty percent) are assigned to types approximately and conditionally, which Nikíforov indicates by brackets.[12] If different investigators begin to attribute the same tale to various types, what will be the result? On the other hand, since types are defined according to the presence of one or another striking incident in them, and not on the basis of the construction of the tales, and since one tale is capable of containing several such incidents, then one tale can sometimes be related to several types at once (up to five numbers for one tale). This does not at all indicate that a given text consists of five tales. Such a method of delineation is, in reality, a definition according to components. For a certain group of tales, Aarne even departs from his principles and quite unexpectedly, and somewhat inconsistently, switches from a division according to themes to a division by motifs. This is the manner in which he designates one of his subclasses, a group which he entitles "About the stupid devil." But this inconsistency again represents an instinctively chosen correct approach. Later I shall try to show that study on the basis of small component parts is the correct method of investigation.

Thus we see that the problem of classification of the tale finds itself in a somewhat sorry state. Yet classification is one of the first and most important steps of study. We need merely recall what a great significance Linnaeus' first scientific classification had for botany. Our studies are still in their "pre-Linnaen" stage.[13]

Let us move on to another most important area of tale investigation: to its factual description. Here we can observe the following picture: very often the investigators, in touching upon questions of description, do not bother with classification (Veselóvskij). On the other hand, classifiers do not always describe a tale in detail, but study only certain aspects of it (Wundt). If an investigator is interested in both approaches, then classification does not follow description, but description is carried on within the framework of a preconceived classification.

Veselóvskij said very little about the description of the tale, but what he did say has enormous significance. Veselóvskij means by "theme" a complex of motifs. A motif can be ascribed to different themes. ("A theme is a series of motifs. A motif develops into a theme." "Themes vary: certain motifs make their way into themes, or else themes combine with one another." "By theme I mean a subject in which various situations, that is, motifs, move in and out."[14]) For Veselóvskij, motif is something primary, theme secondary. A theme is, for him, a creative, unifying act. From this we realize that study must be concerned not so much with themes as with motifs.

Had scholarship concerning the tale acquainted itself better with Veselóvskij's precept—*"separate the question of motifs from the question of themes"* (Veselóvskij's italics)—then many vague matters would already have been done away with.[15]

Yet Veselóvskij's teaching on motifs and themes represents only a general principle. His concrete interpretation of the term "motif" cannot be applied anymore. According to Veselóvskij, a motif is an indivisible narrative unit. ("By the term 'motif' I mean the simplest narrative unit." "The feature of a motif is its figurative, monomial schematism; such are those elements incapable of further decomposition which belong to lower mythology and to the tale.") However, the motifs which he cites as examples do decompose. If a motif is something logically whole, then each sentence of a tale gives a motif. (A father has three sons: a motif; a stepdaughter leaves home: a motif; Iván fights with a dragon: a motif; and so on.) This would not be so bad if motifs were really indivisible; an index of motifs would then be made possible. But let us take the motif "a dragon kidnaps the tsar's daughter" (this example is not Veselóvskij's). This motif decomposes into four elements, each of which, in its own right, can vary. The dragon may be replaced by Koščéj, a whirlwind, a devil, a falcon, or a sorcerer. Abduction can be replaced by vampirism or various other acts by which disappearance is effected in tales. The daughter may be replaced by a sister, a bride, a wife, or a mother. The tsar can be replaced by a tsar's son, a peasant, or a priest. In this way, contrary to Veselóvskij, we must affirm that a motif is not monomial or indivisible. The final divisible unit, as such, does not represent a logical whole. While agreeing with Veselóvskij that a part is more primary for description than the whole (and according to Veselóvskij, a motif is, even by its origin, more primary than the theme), we shall eventually have to solve the problem of the extraction of certain primary elements in a different way than does Veselóvskij.

Other investigators have proved as unsuccessful as Veselóvskij. An example of a methodologically valuable approach can be found in the methods of Bédier.[16] The value of Bédier's methods lies in the fact that he was the first to recognize that some relationship exists in the tale between its constants and variables. He attempts to express this schematically. The constant, essential units he calls *elements*, giving them the sign Ω. He labels the variables with Latin letters. The scheme of one tale, in this manner, gives $\Omega+a+b+c$; another, $\Omega+a+b+c+n$; a third, $\Omega+m+l+n$; and so forth. But his essentially correct idea falls apart in its inability to specify the exact meaning of omega. What Bédier's *elements* are in reality and how to separate them remains unclarified.[17]

The problems of the description of the tale have been relatively neglected in favor of the concept of the tale as something finished, or given. Only at the present time is the idea of the need for an exact description growing ever wider, although the forms of the tale have already long been discussed. And actually, at a time when minerals, plants, and animals are described and classified precisely according to their structure, at a time when a whole range of literary genres (the fable, the ode, drama, etc.) have been described, the tale continues to be studied without such a description. Šklóvskij[18] has shown to what absurdities the so-called genetic studies of the tale have sometimes gone when they fail to consider its forms. As an example he cites the well-known tale about the measurement of land by means of a hide. The hero of the tale obtains permission to take as much land as he is able to encompass with an ox hide. He cuts up the hide into strips and encompasses more land than the deceived party expected. V. F. Míller and others tried to detect here the traces of a judicial act. Šklóvskij writes: "It appears that the deceived party (and in all its variants the tale is concerned with deception) did not protest against the seizure of the land because land was generally measured in this manner. The result is an absurdity. If, at the moment of the supposed performance of the tale's action, the custom of measuring land 'by as much as one can encircle with a belt' existed and was known both to the seller and to the purchaser, then not only is there no deception, but also no theme, since the seller knew what to expect." Thus, the relegation of the story to historical reality, without taking into account the particulars of the story as such, leads to false conclusions, in spite of the investigators' enormous erudition.

The methods of Veselóvskij and Bédier belong to a more or less distant past. Although these scholars worked, in the main, as *historians* of folklore, their methods of formal study represented new achievements which are essentially correct but which have not been worked out or applied by anyone. At the present time the necessity of studying the forms of the tale evokes no objections whatsoever.[19]

Yet present-day scholarship sometimes goes too far in this regard. In the above-mentioned book of Vólkov, one finds the following mode of description: tales first of all decompose into motifs. Qualities of the heroes ("two wise sons-in-law and the third a fool"), their number ("three brothers"), the deeds of heroes ("the injunction of a father for someone to keep watch over his grave after his death, an injunction which is carried out by the fool alone"), objects (a hut on chicken legs, talismans), and so forth, are all considered to be motifs. Each such motif is given a conventional sign—a letter and a number, or a letter and two numbers. More or less similar motifs are marked by one letter with different numbers. At this point just how many motifs does one obtain by being really consistent and marking the entire content of a tale in this way? Vólkov gives about 250 designations (there is no exact listing). It is obvious that there is much omitted and that Vólkov did do some selecting, but how he did it is unknown. Having isolated motifs in this manner, Vólkov proceeds to transcribe tales, mechanically translating motifs into signs and comparing schemes. Similar tales, it is clear, give similar schemes. Transcriptions fill the whole book. The only "conclusion" that can be drawn from this transcription is that similar tales resemble each other—a conclusion which is completely noncommittal and leads nowhere.[20]

We see the nature of the problems investigated by scholars. The less experienced reader may ask: "Doesn't science occupy itself with abstractions which in essence are not at all necessary? Isn't it all the same whether the motif is or is not decomposable? Does it matter how we isolate basic elements, how we classify a tale, and whether we study it according to motifs or themes?" Involuntarily one feels like raising more concrete, tangible questions, questions closer to the average person who simply likes tales. But such a requirement is based on delusion. Let us draw an analogy. Is it possible to speak about the life of a language without knowing anything about the parts of speech, i.e., about certain groups of words arranged according to the laws of their changes? A living language is a concrete fact—grammar is its abstract substratum. These substrata lie at the basis of a great many phenomena of life, and it is precisely to this that science turns its attention. Not a single concrete fact can be explained without the study of these abstract bases.

Scholarship has not limited itself to the problems dealt with here. We have spoken only of those questions related to morphology. In particular, we have not touched upon the enormous field of historical research. This historical research may outwardly be more interesting than morphological investigations, and here a great deal has been done. But the general question of the origin of the tale is, on the whole, unresolved, even though here too there are undoubtedly laws of origin and development which still await elaboration. Instead, all the more has been done on specific questions. The mere enumeration of names and works makes no sense.[21] We shall insist that as long as no correct morphological study exists, there can be no correct historical study. If we are incapable of breaking the tale into its components, we will not be able to make a correct comparison. And if we do not know how to compare, then how can we throw light upon, for instance, Indo-Egyptian relationships, or upon the relationships of the Greek fable to the Indian, etc.? If we cannot compare one tale with another, then how can we compare the tale to religion or to myths? Finally, just as all rivers flow into the sea, all questions relating to the study of tales lead to the solution of the highly important and as yet unresolved problem of the similarity of tales throughout the world. How is one to explain the similarity of the tale about the frog queen in Russia, Germany, France, India, in America among the Indians, and in New Zealand, when the contact of peoples cannot be proven historically? This resemblance cannot be explained if we have wrong conceptions of its character. The historian, inexperienced in morphological problems, will not see a resemblance where one actually exists; he will omit coincidences which are important to him, but which he does not notice. And conversely, where a similarity is perceived, a specialist in morphology will be able to demonstrate that compared phenomena are completely heteronomous.

We see, then, that very much depends upon the study of forms. We shall not refuse to take upon ourselves the crude, analytical, somewhat laborious task which is further complicated by the fact that it is undertaken from the viewpoint of abstract, formal problems. Such crude, "uninteresting" work of this kind is a way to generalize "interesting" constructions.[22]

NOTES

1. M. Speránskij, *Russkaja ustnaja slovesnost'* [*Russian Oral Literature*] (Moscow, 1917, p. 400).

2. J. Bolte and G. Polívka, *Anmerkungen zu den Kinder- und Hausmärchen der Brüder Grimm,* I (1913), II (1915), III (1918).

3. I take this occasion to point out that such an augmentation is possible only through regular international exchange of materials. Although our Union is one of the richest countries of the world in tales, (tales that would be important even if they were only tales of different peoples, in which Mongolian, Indian, and European influences cross), we still do not have a center which would be able to supply necessary information. The Institute of the History of the Arts is organizing an archive for the materials collected by its collaborators. Its transformation into an All-Union archive would have international significance.

4. Cf. Sávčenko, *Russkaja narodnaja skazka* [*The Russian Folktale*] (Kiev, 1913).

5. Proposed by V. F. Míller. This classification in essence coincides with the classification of the mythological school (mythical, about animals, and about daily living).

6. W. Wundt, *Völkerpsychologie,* II, Section I, p. 346 ff.

7. Cf. Lidija Vindt, "Basnja, kak literaturnyj žanr" ["The Fable as a Literary Genre"], *Poètika,* III (Leningrad, 1927).

8. R. M. Vólkov, *Skazka. Rozyskanija po sjužetosloženiju narodnoj skazki.* Vol. I: *Skazka velikorusskaja, ukrainskaja, belorusskaja* [*The Tale. Investigations on the*

Theme Composition of the Folktale. Vol. I: *The Great Russian, Ukrainian, and Belorussian Tale*] (Ukrainian State Publishing House, 1924).

9. A. Aarne, *Verzeichnis der Märchentypen. Folklore Fellows Communications,* No. 3 (Helsinki, 1911).

10. A listing of the works of this school, published under the general title *Folklore Fellows Communications* (abbreviated *FFC*) is given in the first number of the journal *Xudožestvennyj fol'klor,* in the article by N. P. Andreev.

11. Cf. N. P. Andréev's article, "Sistema Aarne i katalogizacija russkix skazok" ["Aarne's System and the Cataloguing of Russian Tales"] in the *Obzor Rabot Skazočnoj Komissii za 1924–25 g.g.* Andreev is preparing a translation of Aarne's index with an application of it to Russian material.

12. A. I. Nikíforov, *Skazočnye materialy Zaonež'ja, sobrannye v 1926 godu* [*Tale Materials of the Trans-Onega Region, Collected in 1926*], in *Obzor Rabot Skazočnoj Komissii za 1926 g.*

13. Our fundamental theses can be further verified by the following classifications: O. Miller in *Opyt istoričeskogo obozrenija russkoj slovesnosti* [*An Experiment in the Historical Survey of Russian Literature*] 2nd ed. (S.P.B., 1865), and in *34-oe prisuždenie Demidovskix nagrad* [*The 34th Awarding of the Demidov Prizes*] (1866); J. G. v. Hahn, *Griechische und albanesische Märchen* (Leipzig, 1864); G. L. Gomme, *The Handbook of Folklore* (London, 1890); P. V. Vladimirov, *Vvedenie v istoriju russkoj slovesnosti* [*Introduction to the History of Russian Literature*] (Kiev, 1896); A. M. Smirnóv, *Sistematičeskij ukazatel' tem i variantov russkix narodnyx skazok* [*A Systematic Index of Themes and Variants of Russian Folktales*] in *Izvestija Otdelenija russkogo jazyka i slovesnosti Akademii Nauk* (XVI–4, XVII–3, XIX–4). Cf. also A. Christensen, *Motif et thème. Plan d'un dictionnaire des motifs de contes populaires, de légendes et de fables,* in *FFC,* No. 59, (Helsinki, 1925).

14. A. N. Veselóvskij, *Poètika* [*Poetics*] Vol. II, Fasc. I: *Poètika sjužetov* [*The Poetics of Themes*]. Introduction, chapters I and II.

15. Vólkov makes a fatal mistake when he says: "The tale's theme is that constant unit from which alone it is possible to proceed to the study of the tale." (*The Tale,* p. 5). We answer: "A theme is not a unit, but a complex, it is not constant, but variable, and one should not proceed from it to the study of the tale."

16. Bédier, *Les Fabliaux* (Paris, 1893).

17. Cf. S. F. Ol'denburg, "Fablio vostočnogo proisxoždenija" ["The Fabliaux of Eastern Origin"] in the *Žurnal Ministerstva Narodnogo Prosveščenija* (October, 1906), in which a more detailed evaluation of Bédier's methods is given.

18. V. Šklóvskij, *Teorija prozy* [*The Theory of Prose*] (Moscow-Leningrad, 1925), p. 24 ff.

19. An article by A. I. Nikíforov, "K voprosu o morfologičeskom izučenii skazki" ["On the Question of the Morphological Study of the Tale"], is being published in the collection in honor of A. I. Sobolévskij.

20. Cf. the reviews of R. Šor (*Pečat' i Revoljucija,* 1924, book 5), S. Savčenko (*Etnohrafičnyj Visnyk,* 1925, book I), and A. I. Nikíforov (*Izvestija Otdelenija russkogo jazyka i slovesnosti Akademii Nauk,* XXXI, 1926, p. 367).

21. Cf. E. Hoffman-Krayer, *Volkskundliche Bibliographie Für das Jahr 1917* (Strassburg, 1919), *Für das Jahr 1918* (Berlin-Leipzig, 1920), *Für das Jahr 1919* (Berlin-Leipzig, 1922). Rich material is presented by the surveys in the *Zeitschrift des Vereins für Volkskunde.*

22. The most important general literature on the tale: W. A. Clouston, *Popular Tales and Fictions, Their Migrations and Transformations* (London, 1887); V. F. Míller, "Vsemirnaja skazka v kul'turno-istoričeskom osveščenii" ["The World-

wide Tale in a Cultural-Historical Interpretation"] (*Russkaja Mysl'*, 1893, XI); R. Koehler, *Aufsätze über Märchen und Volkslieder* (Berlin, 1894); M. G. Xalánskij, "Skazki" ["Tales"], in *Istorija russkoj literatury pod redakciej Aničkova, Borozdina i Ovsjaniko-Kulikovskogo*, Vol. I, Fasc. 2, chap. 6 (Moscow, 1908); A. Thimme, *Das Märchen* (Leipzig, 1909); A. Van Gennep, *La formation des légendes* (Paris, 1910); F. v.d. Leyen, *Das Märchen*, 2nd ed. (1917); K. Spiess, "Das deutsche Volksmärchen," in *Aus Natur und Geisteswelt*, Fasc. 587 (Leipzig and Berlin, 1917); S. F. Ol'denburg, "Stranstvovanie skazki" ["The Wandering of the Tale"] in *Vostok*, no. 4; G. Huet, *Les contes populaires* (Paris, 1923).

CHAPTER II

The Method and Material

Let us first of all attempt to formulate our task. As already stated in the foreword, this work is dedicated to the study of *fairy* tales. The existence of fairy tales as a special class is assumed as an essential working hypothesis. By "fairy tales" are meant at present those tales classified by Aarne under numbers 300 to 749. This definition is artificial, but the occasion will subsequently arise to give a more precise determination on the basis of resultant conclusions. We are undertaking a comparison of the themes of these tales. For the sake of comparison we shall separate the component parts of fairy tales by special methods; and then, we shall make a comparison of tales according to their components. The result will be a morphology (i.e., a description of the tale according to its component parts and the relationship of these components to each other and to the whole).

What methods can achieve an accurate description of the tale? Let us compare the following events:

1. A tsar gives an eagle to a hero. The eagle carries the hero away to another kingdom.†
2. An old man gives Súčenko a horse. The horse carries Súčenko away to another kingdom.

† *"Car' daet udal'cu orla. Orel unosit udal'ca v inoe carstvo"* (p. 28). Actually, in the tale referred to (old number 104a = new number 171), the hero's future bride, Poljuša, tells her father the tsar that they have a *ptica-kolpalica* (technically a spoonbill, although here it may have meant a white stork), which can carry them to the bright world. For a tale in which the hero flies away on an eagle, see 71a (= new number 128). [L.A.W.]

3. A sorcerer gives Iván a little boat. The boat takes Iván to another kingdom.
4. A princess gives Iván a ring. Young men appearing from out of the ring carry Iván away into another kingdom, and so forth.[1]

Both constants and variables are present in the preceding instances. The names of the dramatis personae change (as well as the attributes of each), but neither their actions nor functions change. From this we can draw the inference that a tale often attributes identical actions to various personages. This makes possible the study of the tale *according to the functions of its dramatis personae.*

We shall have to determine to what extent these functions actually represent recurrent constants of the tale. The formulation of all other questions will depend upon the solution of this primary question: how many functions are known to the tale?

Investigation will reveal that the recurrence of functions is astounding. Thus Bába Jagá, Morózko, the bear, the forest spirit, and the mare's head test and reward the stepdaughter. Going further, it is possible to establish that characters of a tale, however varied they may be, often perform the same actions. The actual means of the realization of functions can vary, and as such, it is a variable. Morózko behaves differently than Bába Jagá. But the function, as such, is a constant. The question of *what* a tale's dramatis personae do is an important one for the study of the tale, but the questions of *who* does it and *how* it is done already fall within the province of accessory study. The functions of characters are those components which could replace Veselóvskij's "motifs," or Bédier's "elements." We are aware of the fact that the repetition of functions by various characters was long ago observed in myths and beliefs by historians of religion, but it was not observed by historians of the tale (cf. Wundt and Negelein[2]). Just as the characteristics and functions of deities are transferred from one to another, and, finally, are even carried over to Christian saints, the functions of certain tale personages are likewise transferred to other personages. Running ahead, one may say that the number of functions is extremely small, whereas the number of personages is extremely large. This explains the two-fold quality of a tale: its amazing multiformity, picturesqueness, and color, and on the other hand, its no less striking uniformity, its repetition.

Thus the functions of the dramatis personae are basic components of the tale, and we must first of all extract them. In order to extract the functions we must define them. Definition must proceed from two points of view. First of all, definition should in no case depend on the personage who carries out the function. Definition of a function will most often be given in the form of a noun expressing an action (interdiction, interrogation, flight, etc.). Secondly, an action cannot be defined apart from its place in the course of narration. The meaning which a given function has in the course of action must be considered. For example, if Iván marries a tsar's daughter, this is something entirely different than the marriage of a father to a widow with two daughters. A second example: if, in one instance, a hero receives money from his father in the form of 100 rubles and subsequently buys a wise cat with this money, whereas in a second case, the hero is rewarded with a sum of money for an accomplished act of bravery (at which point the tale ends), we have before us two morphologically different elements—in spite of the identical action (the transference of money) in both cases. Thus, identical acts can have different meanings, and vice versa. *Function is understood as an act of a character, defined from the point of view of its significance for the course of the action.*

The observations cited may be briefly formulated in the following manner:

1. *Functions of characters serve as stable, constant elements in a tale, independent of how and by whom they are fulfilled. They constitute the fundamental components of a tale.*
2. *The number of functions known to the fairy tale is limited.*

If functions are delineated, a second question arises: in what classification and in what sequence are these functions encountered?

A word, first, about sequence. The opinion exists that this sequence is accidental. Veselóvskij writes, "The selection and *order* of tasks and encounters (examples of motifs) already presupposes a certain *freedom.*" Šklóvskij stated this idea in even sharper terms: "It is quite impossible to understand why, in the act of adoption, the *accidental* sequence [Šklóvskij's italics] of motifs must be retained. In the testimony of witnesses, it is precisely the sequence of events which is distorted most of all." This reference to the evidence of witnesses is unconvincing. If witnesses distort the sequence of events, their narration is meaningless. The sequence of events has its own laws. The short story too has similar laws, as do organic formations. Theft cannot take place before the door is forced. Insofar as the tale is concerned, it has its own entirely particular and specific laws. The sequence of elements, as we shall see later on, is strictly *uniform*. Freedom within this sequence is restricted by very narrow limits which can be exactly formulated. We thus obtain the third basic thesis of this work, subject to further development and verification:

3. *The sequence of functions is always identical.*

As for groupings, it is necessary to say first of all that by no means do all tales give evidence of all functions. But this in no way changes the law of sequence. The absence of certain functions does not change the order of the rest. We shall dwell on this phenomenon later. For the present we shall deal with groupings in the proper sense of the word. The presentation of the question itself evokes the following assumption: if functions are singled out, then it will be possible to trace those tales which present identical functions. Tales with identical functions can be considered as belonging to one type. On this foundation, an index of types can then be created, based not upon theme features, which are somewhat vague and diffuse, but upon exact structural features. Indeed, this will be possible. If we further compare structural types among themselves, we are led to the following completely unexpected phenomenon: functions cannot be distributed around mutually exclusive axes. This phenomenon, in all its concreteness, will become apparent to us in the succeeding and final chapters of this book. For the time being, it can be interpreted in the following manner: if we designate with the letter A a function encountered everywhere in first position, and similarly designate with the letter B the function which (if it is at all present) *always follows A*, then all functions known to the tale will arrange themselves within a *single* tale, and none will fall out of order, nor will any one exclude or contradict any other. This is, of course, a completely unexpected result. Naturally, we would have expected that where there is a function A, there cannot be certain functions belonging to other tales. Supposedly we would obtain several axes, but only a single axis is obtained for all fairy tales. They are of the same type, while the combinations spoken of previously are subtypes. At first glance, this conclusion may appear absurd or perhaps even wild, yet it can be verified in a most exact manner. Such a typological unity represents a very complex problem on which it will be necessary to dwell further. This phenomenon will raise a whole series of questions.

In this manner, we arrive at the fourth basic thesis of our work:

4. *All fairy tales are of one type in regard to their structure.*

We shall now set about the task of proving, developing, and elaborating these theses in detail. Here it should be recalled that the study of the tale must be carried on strictly deductively, i.e., proceeding from the material at hand to the consequences (and in effect it is so carried on in this work). But the *presentation* may have a reversed order, since it is easier to follow the development if the general bases are known to the reader beforehand.

Before starting the elaboration, however, it is necessary to decide what material can serve as the subject of this study. First glance would seem to indicate that it is necessary to cover all extant material. In fact, this is not so. Since we are studying tales according to the functions of their dramatis personae, the accumulation of material can be suspended as soon as it becomes apparent that the new tales considered present no new functions. Of course, the investigator must look through an enormous amount of reference material. But there is no need to inject the entire body of this material into the study. We have found that 100 tales constitute more than enough material. Having discovered that no new functions can be found, the morphologist can put a stop to his work, and further study will follow different directions (the formation of indices, the complete systemization, historical study). But just because material can be limited in quantity, that does not mean that it can be selected at one's own discretion. It should be dictated from without. We shall use the collection by Afanás'ev, starting the study of tales with No. 50 (according to his plan, this is the first fairy tale of the collection), and finishing it with No. 151.† Such a limitation of material will undoubtedly call forth many objections, but it is theoretically justified. To justify it further, it would be necessary to take into account the degree of repetition of tale phenomena. If repetition is great, then one may take a limited amount of material. If repetition is small, this is impossible. The repetition of fundamental components, as we shall see later, exceeds all expectations. Consequently, it is theoretically possible to limit oneself to a small body of material. Practically, this limitation justifies itself by the fact that the inclusion of a great quantity of material would have excessively increased the size of this work. We are not interested in the quantity of material, but in the quality of its analysis. Our working material consists of 100 tales. The rest is reference material, of great interest to the investigator, but lacking a broader interest.

† Tales numbered 50 to 151 refer to enumeration according to the older editions of Afanás'ev. In the new system of enumeration, adopted for the fifth and sixth editions and utilized in this translation (cf. the Preface to the Second Edition, and Appendix V), the corresponding numbers are 93 to 270. [L.A.W.]

NOTES

1. See Afanás'ev, Nos. 171, 139, 138, 156.
2. W. Wundt, "Mythus und Religion," *Völkerpsychologie,* II, Section I; Negelein, *Germanische Mythologie*. Negelein creates an exceptionally apt term, *Depossedierte Gottheiten*.

CHAPTER III

The Functions of Dramatis Personae

In this chapter we shall enumerate the functions of the dramatis personae in the order dictated by the tale itself.

For each function there is given: (1) a brief summary of its essence, (2) an abbreviated definition in one word, and (3) its conventional sign. (The introduction of signs will later permit a schematic comparison of the structure of various tales.) Then follow examples. For the most part, the examples far from exhaust our material. They are given only as samples. They are distributed into certain groups. These groups are in relation to the definition as *species* to *genus*. The basic task is the extraction of *genera*. An examination of *species* cannot be included in the problems of general morphology. Species can be further subdivided into *varieties,* and here we have the beginning of systemization. The arrangement given below does not pursue such goals. The citation of examples should only illustrate and show the presence of the function as a certain *generic* unit. As was already mentioned, all functions fit into one consecutive story. The series of functions given below represents the morphological foundation of fairy tales in general.[1]

A tale usually begins with some sort of initial situation. The members of a family are enumerated, or the future hero (e.g., a soldier) is simply introduced by mention of his name or indication of his status. Although this situation is not a function, it nevertheless is an important morphological element. The species of tale beginnings can be examined only at the end of the present work. We shall designate this element as the *initial situation,* giving it the sign α.

After the initial situation there follow functions:

I. ONE OF THE MEMBERS OF A FAMILY ABSENTS HIMSELF FROM HOME. (Definition: *absentation.* Designation: β.)

1. *The person absenting himself can be a member of the older generation* (β^1). Parents leave for work (113). "The prince had to go on a distant journey, leaving his wife to the care of strangers" (265). "Once, he (a merchant) went away to foreign lands" (197). Usual forms of absentation: going to work, to the forest, to trade, to war, "on business."
2. *An intensified form of absentation is represented by the death of parents* (β^2).
3. *Sometimes members of the younger generation absent themselves* (β^3). They go visiting (101), fishing (108), for a walk (137), out to gather berries (244).

II. AN INTERDICTION IS ADDRESSED TO THE HERO. (Definition: *interdiction.* Designation: γ.)

1. (γ^1). "You dare not look into this closet" (159). "Take care of your little brother, do not venture forth from the courtyard" (113). "If Bába Jagá comes, don't you say anything, be silent" (106). "Often did the prince try to persuade her and command her not to leave the lofty tower," etc. (265). Interdiction not to go out is sometimes strengthened or replaced by putting children in a stronghold (201). Sometimes, on the contrary, an interdiction is evidenced in a weakened form, as a request or bit of advice: a mother tries to persuade her son not to go out fishing: "you're still little," etc. (108). The tale generally mentions an absentation at first, and then an interdiction. The sequence of events, of course, actually runs in the reverse. Interdictions can also be made without being connected with an absentation: "don't pick the apples" (230); "don't pick up the golden feather" (169); "don't open the chest" (219); "don't kiss your sister" (219).

2. *An inverted form of interdiction is represented by an order or a suggestion.* (γ^2) "Bring breakfast out into the field" (133). "Take your brother with you to the woods" (244).

Here for the sake of better understanding, a digression may be made. Further on the tale presents the sudden arrival of calamity (but not without a certain type of preparation). In connection with this, the initial situation gives a description of particular, sometimes emphasized, prosperity. A tsar has a wonderful garden with golden apples; the old folk fondly love their Ivášečka, and so on. A particular form is agrarian prosperity: a peasant and his sons have a wonderful hay-making. One often encounters the description of sowing with excellent germination. This prosperity naturally serves as a contrasting background for the misfortune to follow. The spectre of this misfortune already hovers invisibly above the happy family. From this situation stem the interdictions not to go out into the street, and others. The very absentation of elders prepares for the misfortune, creating an opportune moment for it. Children, after the departure or death of their parents, are left on their own. A command often plays the role of an interdiction. If children are urged to go out into the field or into the forest, the fulfillment of this command has the same consequences as does violation of an interdiction not to go into the forest or out into the field.

III. THE INTERDICTION IS VIOLATED (Definition: *violation.* Designation: δ.)

The forms of violation correspond to the forms of interdiction. Functions II and III form a *paired* element. The second half can sometimes exist without the first (the tsar's daughters go into the garden [β^3]; they are *late* in returning home). Here the interdiction of tardiness is omitted. A fulfilled order corresponds, as demonstrated, to a violated interdiction.

At this point a new personage, who can be termed the *villain,* enters the tale. His role is to disturb the peace of a happy family, to cause some form of misfortune, damage, or harm. The villain(s) may be a dragon, a devil, bandits, a witch, or a stepmother, etc. (The question of how new personages, in general, appear in the course of action has been relegated to a special chapter.) Thus, a villain has entered the scene. He has come on foot, sneaked up, or flown down, etc., and begins to act.

IV. THE VILLAIN MAKES AN ATTEMPT AT RECONNAISSANCE. (Definition: *reconnaissance*. Designation: ε.)

1. *The reconnaissance has the aim of finding out the location of children, or sometimes of precious objects, etc.* (ε^1). A bear says: "Who will tell me what has become of the tsar's children? Where did they disappear to?" (201); a clerk: "Where do you get these precious stones?" (197); † a priest at confession: "How were you able to get well so quickly?" (258); †† a princess: "Tell me, Iván the merchant's son, where is your wisdom?" (209);††† "What does the bitch live on?" Jágišna thinks. She sends One-Eye, Two-Eye and Three-Eye on reconnaissance (101).‡
2. *An inverted form of reconnaissance is evidenced when the intended victim questions the villain* (ε^2). "Where is your death, Koščéj?" (156). "What a swift steed you have! Could one get another one somewhere that could outrun yours?" (160).
3. *In separate instances one encounters forms of reconnaissance by means of other personages* (ε^3).

V. THE VILLAIN RECEIVES INFORMATION ABOUT HIS VICTIM. (Definition: *delivery*. Designation: ζ.)

1. *The villain directly receives an answer to his question.* (ζ^1) The chisel answers the bear: "Take me out into the courtyard and throw me to the ground; where

† " 'Gde vy èti samocvetnye kamni berete?' (114)" (p. 38). The textual reference should be 115 (= new no. 197). [L.A.W.]

†† " 'Otčego tak skoro suṃel ty popraṿit'sja?' (114)" (p. 38). The textual reference should be 144 (= new no. 258). [L.A.W.]

††† " 'Skaži, Ivan—kupečeskij syn, gde tvoja mudrost'?' (120)" (p. 38). The textual reference should be 120b (= new no. 209). [L.A.W.]

‡ " 'Čem suka živet? dumaet Jagišna.' Ona posylaet na razvedku Odnoglazku, Dvuglazku, Treglazku (56)." Texts 56 and 57 (= new nos. 100 and 101) have been somewhat confused. The three daughters named are present in tale 56, but their mother is not called Jagišna, and the indicated question does not appear. On the other hand, in tale 57 Jagišna asks, "Čem suka živa živet?" but here she has only two daughters to send out, a two-eyed one and a three-eyed one. [L.A.W.]

I stick, there's the hive." To the clerk's question about the precious stones, the merchant's wife replies: "Oh, the hen lays them for us," etc. Once again we are confronted with paired functions. They often occur in the form of a dialogue. Here, incidentally, also belongs the dialogue between the stepmother and the mirror. Although the stepmother does not directly ask about her stepdaughter, the mirror answers her: "There is no doubt of your beauty; but you have a stepdaughter, living with knights in the deep forest, and she is even more beautiful." As in other similar instances, the second half of the paired function can exist without the first. In these cases the delivery takes the form of a careless act: A mother calls her son home in a loud voice and thereby betrays his presence to a witch (108). An old man has received a marvelous bag; he gives the godmother a treat from the bag and thereby gives away the secret of his talisman to her (187).

2–3. *An inverted or other form of information-gathering evokes a corresponding answer.* (ζ^2-ζ^3) Koščéj reveals the secret of his death (156), the secret of the swift steed (159), and so forth.

VI. THE VILLAIN ATTEMPTS TO DECEIVE HIS VICTIM IN ORDER TO TAKE POSSESSION OF HIM OR OF HIS BELONGINGS. (Definition: *trickery*. Designation: η.)

The villain, first of all, assumes a disguise. A dragon turns into a golden goat (162), or a handsome youth (204);† a witch pretends to be a "sweet old lady" (265) and imitates a mother's voice (108); a priest dresses himself in a goat's hide (258); a thief pretends to be a beggarwoman (189). Then follows the function itself.

1. *The villain uses persuasion* (η^1). A witch tries to have a ring accepted (114); a godmother suggests the taking of a steam bath (187); a witch suggests the removal of clothes (264) and bathing in a pond (265); a beggar seeks alms (189).

† The tale reference cited (p. 39) is 118. More specifically, it should be 118c (= new no. 204). [L.A.W.]

2. *The villain proceeds to act by the direct application of magical means* (η^2). The stepmother gives a sleeping potion to her stepson. She sticks a magic pin into his clothing (232).

3. *The villain employs other means of deception or coercion* (η^3). Evil sisters place knives and spikes around a window through which Finist is supposed to fly (234). A dragon rearranges the wood shavings that are to show a young girl the way to her brothers (133).

VII. THE VICTIM SUBMITS TO DECEPTION AND THEREBY UNWITTINGLY HELPS HIS ENEMY. (Definition: *complicity*. Designation: θ.)

1. *The hero agrees to all of the villain's persuasions* (i.e., takes the ring, goes to steambathe, to swim, etc.). One notes that *interdictions* are always *broken* and, conversely, *deceitful proposals* are always *accepted* and fulfilled (θ^1).

2–3. *The hero mechanically reacts to the employment of magical or other means* (i.e., falls asleep, wounds himself, etc.). It can be observed that this function can also exist separately. No one lulls the hero to sleep: he suddenly falls asleep by himself in order, of course, to facilitate the villain's task (θ^2-θ^3).

A special form of deceitful proposal and its corresponding acceptance is represented by the deceitful agreement. ("Give away that which you do not know you have in your house.") Assent in these instances is compelled, the villain taking advantage of some difficult situation in which his victim is caught: a scattered flock, extreme poverty, etc. Sometimes the difficult situation is deliberately caused by the villain. (The bear seizes the tsar by the beard [201]). This element may be defined as *preliminary misfortune*. (Designation: λ, differentiating between this and other forms of deception.)

VIII. THE VILLAIN CAUSES HARM OR INJURY TO A MEMBER OF A FAMILY. (Definition: *villainy*. Designation: A.)

This function is exceptionally important, since by means of it the actual movement of the tale is created. Absentation, the violation of an interdiction, delivery, the success of a deceit, all prepare the way for this function, create its possibility of occurrence, or simply facilitate its happening. Therefore, the first seven functions may be regarded as the *preparatory part* of the tale, whereas the complication is begun by an act of villainy. The forms of villainy are exceedingly varied.

1. *The villain abducts a person* (A^1). A dragon kidnaps the tsar's daughter (131),† a peasant's daughter (133); a witch kidnaps a boy (108); older brothers abduct the bride of a younger brother (168).

2. *The villain seizes or takes away a magical agent* (A^2). The "uncomely chap" seizes a magic coffer (189); †† a princess seizes a magic shirt (208); the finger-sized peasant makes off with a magic steed (138).

   2a. The forcible seizure of a magical helper creates a special subclass of this form (A^{II}). A stepmother orders the killing of a miraculous cow (100, 101). A clerk orders the slaying of a magic duck or chicken (196, 197).†††

3. *The villain pillages or spoils the crops* (A^3). A mare eats up a haystack (105). A bear steals the oats (143). A crane steals the peas (186).

4. *The villain seizes the daylight* (A^4). This occurs only once (135).

5. *The villain plunders in other forms* (A^5). The object of seizure fluctuates to an enormous degree, and there is no need to register all of its forms. The object of plunder, as will be apparent later on, does not influence the course of action. Logically, it would generally be more correct to consider all seizure as *one form* of villainy, and all constituent forms of seizure (subdivided according to their objects) not as classes, but as subclasses. Nevertheless, it is technically more useful to

† "Zmej poxiščaet doč' carja (72). . ." (p. 40). More accurately, the dragon suddenly kidnaps the tsar's three daughters. [L.A.W.]

†† " 'Nevzdrašnyj detinka' poxiščaet volšebnyj larec (111)" (p. 41). In the text cited, the fellow does not steal the coffer himself; he has his mother steal it and bring it to him. [L.A.W.]

††† The original references (on p. 41) are to tales 114 and 115. Tale 114 should be 114b (= new no. 196). [L.A.W.]

isolate several of its most important forms, and generalize the remainder. Examples: a firebird steals the golden apples (168); a weasel-beast each night eats animals from the tsar's menagerie (132); the general seizes the king's (nonmagical) sword (259); and so forth.

6. *The villain causes bodily injury* (A^6). A servant girl cuts out the eyes of her mistress (127). A princess chops off Katóma's legs (198). It is interesting that these forms (from a morphological point of view) are also forms of seizure. The eyes, for example, are placed by the servant girl in a pocket and are carried away; thus they are consequently acquired in the same manner as other seized objects and are put in their proper place. The same is true for a heart that has been cut out.

7. *The villain causes a sudden disappearance* (A^7). Usually this disappearance is the result of the application of bewitching or deceitful means; a stepmother puts her stepson into a sleep—his bride disappears forever (232).† Sisters place knives and needles in a maiden's window through which Finist is supposed to fly in—he injures his wings and disappears forever (234).†† A wife flies away from her husband upon a magic carpet (192). Tale No. 267 demonstrates an interesting form. There, disappearance is effected by the hero himself: he burns the (outer) skin of his bewitched wife, and she disappears forever.††† A special occurrence in tale No. 219 might also conditionally be placed in this class: a bewitched kiss causes a prince to completely forget his bride. In this case the victim is the bride, who loses her betrothed (A^{vii}).

8. *The villain demands or entices his victim* (A^8). Usu-

† "Ego nevesta isčezaet navsegda (128)" (p. 42). The word "forever" may suggest the wrong idea. In reality, the bride leaves a letter for the sleeping hero after her last appearance, saying that he must come and seek her beyond the thrice-ninth kingdom. He does find her eventually, and then marries her. [L.A.W.]

†† "On ranit sebe kryl'ja, isčezaet navsegda (129)" (p. 42). Here again, even though Finist no longer flies to the maiden's window, she sets out after him, finds him, and they are finally married. [L.A.W.]

††† The beautiful wife, fated to wear a frog's skin, takes it off in order to attend a ball. Prince Iván finds the skin and burns it. Here too, although the wife disappears the next morning, it is not "forever" (". . . ona isčezaet navsegda" [p. 42]), as the hero seeks her out again. [L.A.W.]

ally this form is the result of a deceitful agreement. The king of the sea demands the tsar's son, and he leaves home (219).

9. *The villain expels someone* (A^{9}): A stepmother drives her stepdaughter out (95); a priest expels his grandson (143).

10. *The villain orders someone to be thrown into the sea* (A^{10}). A tsar places his daughter and son-in-law in a barrel and orders the barrel to be thrown into the sea (165). Parents launch a small boat, carrying their sleeping son, into the sea (247).

11. *The villain casts a spell upon someone or something* (A^{11}). At this point one should note that the villain often causes two or three harmful acts at once. There are forms which are rarely encountered independently and which show a propensity for uniting with other forms. The casting of spells belongs to this group. A wife turns her husband into a dog and then drives him out (i.e., A_{11}^{9}); a stepmother turns her stepdaughter into a lynx and drives her out (266). Even in instances when a bride is changed into a duck and flies away, we actually have a case of expulsion, although it is not mentioned as such (264, 265).

12. *The villain effects a substitution* (A^{12}). This form also is mostly concomitant. A nursemaid changes a bride into a duckling and substitutes her own daughter in the bride's place (A_{12}^{11}; 264). A maid blinds the tsar's bride and poses as the bride (A_{12}^{6}; 127).

13. *The villain orders a murder to be committed* (A^{13}). This form is in essence a modified (intensified) expulsion: the stepmother orders a servant to kill her stepdaughter while they are out walking (210). A princess orders her servants to take her husband away into the forest and kill him (192). Usually in such instances a presentation of the heart and liver of the victim is demanded.

14. *The villain commits murder* (A^{14}). This also is usually only an accompanying form for other acts of villainy, serving to intensify them. A princess seizes her husband's magic shirt and then kills him (i.e., A_{14}^{2};

209).† Elder brothers kill a younger brother and abduct his bride (i.e., A_{14}^{1}; 168). A sister takes away her brother's berries and then kills him (244).

15. *The villain imprisons or detains someone* (A^{15}). The princess imprisons Iván in a dungeon (185). The king of the sea incarcerates Semën (259).††

16. *The villain threatens forced matrimony* (A^{16}). A dragon demands the tsar's daughter as his wife (125).

16a. The same form among relatives (A^{xvi}). A brother demands his sister for a wife (114).

17. *The villain makes a threat of cannibalism* (A^{17}). A dragon demands the tsar's daughter for his dinner (171). A dragon has devoured all the people in the village, and the last living peasant is threatened with the same fate (149).†††

17a. The same form among relatives (A^{xvii}). A sister intends to devour her brother (93).

18. *The villain torments at night* (A^{18}). A dragon (192) or a devil (115) torment a princess at night; a witch flies to a maiden and sucks at her breast (198).

19. *The villain declares war* (A^{19}). A neighboring tsar declares war (161); similarly, a dragon ravages kingdoms (137).

With this, the forms of villainy are exhausted within the confines of the selected material. However, far from all tales begin with the affliction of misfortune. There are also other beginnings which often present the same development as tales which begin with (A). On examining this phenomenon, we can observe that these tales proceed from a certain situation of insufficiency or lack, and it is this that leads to quests analogous to those in the case of villainy. We conclude from this that lack can be considered as the morphological equivalent of seizure, for example. Let us consider the following cases: a princess seizes Iván's talis-

† The tale reference cited (p. 43) is 120. More correctly, it should be 120b (= new no. 209). [L.A.W.]

†† "Morskoj car' deržit v zatočenii Semena (142)" (p. 43). This does not occur in tale 142. However, it may be found in tale 145 (= new no. 259). [L.A.W.]

††† "Zmej požral vsex ljudej v derevne, ta že učast' ugrožaet poslednemu ostavšemusja v živyx mužiku (85)" (p. 43). This is not the situation in tale 85, but it is in tale 86 (= new no. 149). [L.A.W.]

man. The result of this seizure is that Iván lacks the talisman. And so we see that a tale, while omitting villainy, very often begins directly with a lack: Iván desires to have a magic sabre or a magic steed, etc. Insufficiency, just as seizure, determines the next point of the complication: Iván sets out on a quest. The same may be said about the abduction of a bride as about the simple lack of a bride. In the first instance a certain act is given, the result of which creates an insufficiency and provokes a quest; in the second instance a ready-made insufficiency is presented, which also provokes a quest. In the first instance, a lack is created from without; in the second, it is realized from within.

We fully admit that the terms "lack" (*nedostáča*) and "insufficiency" (*nexvátka*) are not wholly satisfactory. But there are no words in the Russian language with which the given concept may be expressed completely and exactly. The word "shortage" (*nedostátok*) sounds better, but it has a special meaning which is inappropriate for the given concept. This lack can be compared to the zero which, in a series of figures, represents a definite value. The given feature may be fixed in the following manner:

VIIIa. ONE MEMBER OF A FAMILY EITHER LACKS SOMETHING OR DESIRES TO HAVE SOMETHING. (Definition: *lack*. Designation: *a*.)

These instances lend themselves to a grouping only with difficulty. It would be possible to break them down according to the forms of the realization of lack (see pages 53–55); but here it is possible to limit oneself to a distribution according to the objects lacking. It is possible to register the following forms: (1) Lack of a bride (or a friend, or a human being generally). This lack is sometimes depicted quite vividly (the hero intends to search for a bride), and sometimes it is not even mentioned verbally. The hero is unmarried and sets out to find a bride—with this a beginning is given to the course of the action (a^1). (2) A magical agent is needed. For example: apples, water, horses, sabres, etc. (a^2).[2] (3) *Wondrous* objects are lacking (without magical power), such as the firebird, ducks with golden feathers, a wonder-of-wonders, etc. (a^3). (4) A specific form: the magic egg containing Koščéj's death (or containing the love of a princess) is lacking (a^4). (5) Rationalized forms: money, the means of existence, etc. are lacking (a^5). We note that such beginnings from daily living sometimes develop quite fantastically. (6) Various other forms (a^6).

Just as the object of seizure does not determine the structure of the tale, neither does the object which is lacking. In consequence, there is no need to systematize all instances for the sake of the general goals of morphology. One can limit oneself to the most important ones and generalize the rest.

Here the following problem necessarily arises: far from all tales begin with harm or the beginning just described. The tale of Emélja the Fool begins with the fool's catching a pike, and not at all with villainy, etc. In comparing a large number of tales it becomes apparent, however, that the elements peculiar to the *middle* of the tale are sometimes *transferred to the beginning,* and this is the case here. The catching and sparing of an animal is a typical middle element, as we shall observe later on. Generally, elements A or *a* are required for each tale of the class being studied. Other forms of complication do not exist.

IX. MISFORTUNE OR LACK IS MADE KNOWN; THE HERO IS APPROACHED WITH A REQUEST OR COMMAND; HE IS ALLOWED TO GO OR HE IS DISPATCHED. (Definition: *mediation, the connective incident.* Designation: B.)

This function brings the hero into the tale. Under the closest analysis, this function may be subdivided into components, but for our purposes this is not essential. The hero of the tale may be one of two types: (1) if a young girl is kidnapped, and disappears from the horizon of her father (and that of the listener), and if Iván goes off in search of her, then the hero of the tale is Iván and not the kidnapped girl. Heroes of this type may be termed *seekers.* (2) If a young girl or boy is seized or driven out, and the thread of the narrative is linked to his or her fate and not to those who remain behind, then the hero of the tale is the seized or banished boy or girl. There are no seekers in such tales. Heroes of this variety may be called *victimized heroes.*[3] Whether or not tales develop in the same manner with each type of hero will be apparent further on. There is no instance in our material in which a tale follows both seeker and victimized heroes (cf. "Ruslán and Ljudmíla"). A moment of mediation is present in both cases. The significance of this moment lies in the fact that the hero's departure from home is caused by it.

1. *A call for help is given, with the resultant dispatch of the hero* (B^1). The call usually comes from the tsar and is accompanied by promises.
2. *The hero is dispatched directly* (B^2). Dispatch is presented either in the form of a command or a request. In the former instance, it is sometimes accompanied by threats; in the latter, by promises. Sometimes both threats and promises are made.
3. *The hero is allowed to depart from home* (B^3). In this instance the initiative for departure often comes from the hero himself, and not from a dispatcher. Parents bestow their blessing. The hero sometimes does not announce his real aims for leaving: he asks for permission to go out walking, etc., but in reality he is setting off for the struggle.
4. *Misfortune is announced* (B^4). A mother tells her son about the abduction of her daughter that took place before his birth. The son sets out in search of his sister, without having been asked to do so by his mother (133). More often, however, a story of misfortune does not come from parents, but rather from various old women or persons casually encountered, etc.

These four preceding forms all refer to seeker-heroes. The forms following are directly related to the victimized hero. The structure of the tale demands that the hero leave home at any cost. If this is not accomplished by means of some form of villainy, then the tale employs the connective incident to this end.

5. *The banished hero is transported away from home* (B^5): The father takes his daughter, banished by her stepmother, to the forest. This form is quite interesting in many respects. Logically, the father's actions are not necessary. The daughter could go to the forest herself. But the tale demands parent-senders in the connective incident. It is possible to show that the form in question is a secondary formation, but this is outside the aim of a general morphology. One should take note of the fact

that transportation is also employed in regard to a princess who is demanded by a dragon. In such cases she is taken to the seashore. However, in the latter instance a call for help is concurrently given. The course of action is determined by the call and not by transportation to the seashore. This explains why transportation in these instances cannot be attributed to the connective incident.

6. *The hero condemned to death is secretly freed* (B^6). A cook or an archer spares a young girl (or boy), frees her, and instead of killing her, slays an animal in order to obtain its heart and liver as proof of the murder (210, 197).† Incident B was defined above as the factor causing the departure of the hero from home. Whereas dispatch presents the *necessity* for setting out, here the *opportunity* for departure is given. The first instance is characteristic of the seeker-hero, and the second applies to the victimized hero.

7. *A lament is sung* (B^7). This form is specific for murder (and is sung by a surviving brother, etc.); it is specific for bewitchment with banishment, and for substitution. The misfortune becomes known, thanks to this, and evokes counteraction.

X. THE SEEKER AGREES TO OR DECIDES UPON COUNTERACTION. (Definition: *beginning counteraction.* Designation: C.)

This moment is characterized in such words, for instance, as the following: "Permit us to go in search of your princess", etc. Sometimes this moment is not expressed in words, but a volitional decision, of course, precedes the search. This moment is characteristic only of those tales in which the hero is a seeker. Banished, vanquished, bewitched, and substituted heroes demonstrate no volitional aspiration toward freedom, and in such cases this element is lacking.

† The original textual citations (p. 47) for this situation are tales 121 and 114. It does occur in both 121a and 121b, but not in either 114a or 114b. A correct reference to replace the second would be 115 (= new no. 197). [L.A.W.]

XI. THE HERO LEAVES HOME. (Definition: *departure*. Designation: ↑.)

Departure here denotes something different from the temporary absence element, designated earlier by β. The departures of seeker-heroes and victim-heroes are also different. The departures of the former group have search as their goal, while those of the latter mark the beginning of a journey without searches, on which various adventures await the hero. It is necessary to keep the following in mind: if a young girl is abducted and a seeker goes in pursuit of her, then two characters have left home. But the route followed by the story and on which the action is developed is actually the route of the seeker. If, for example, a girl is driven out and there is no seeker, then the narrative is developed along the route of the victim hero. The sign ↑ designates the route of the hero, regardless of whether he is a seeker or not. In certain tales a spatial transference of the hero is absent. The entire action takes place in one location. Sometimes, on the contrary, departure is intensified, assuming the character of flight.

The elements ABC ↑ represent the complication. Later on the course of action is developed.

Now a new character enters the tale: this personage might be termed the *donor,* or more precisely, the provider. Usually he is encountered accidentally—in the forest, along the roadway, etc. (see Chapter VI, forms of appearance of dramatis personae). It is from him that the hero (both the seeker hero and the victim hero) obtains some agent (usually magical) which permits the eventual liquidation of misfortune. But before receipt of the magical agent takes place, the hero is subjected to a number of quite diverse actions which, however, all lead to the result that a magical agent comes into his hands.

XII. THE HERO IS TESTED, INTERROGATED, ATTACKED, ETC., WHICH PREPARES THE WAY FOR HIS RECEIVING EITHER A MAGICAL AGENT OR HELPER. (Definition: *the first function of the donor*. Designation: D.)

1. *The donor tests the hero* (D^1). A witch gives a girl household chores (102). Forest knights propose that the hero serve them for three years. The hero is to spend

three years in the service of a merchant (a rationalization from domestic life) (115). The hero is supposed to serve as a ferryman for three years, without remuneration (138).† The hero must listen to the playing of the gusla without falling asleep (216). The apple tree, the river, and the stove offer a very simple meal (113). A witch proposes bedding down with her daughter (171). A dragon suggests the raising of a heavy stone (128). Sometimes this request is written on the stone, and other times brothers, upon finding a big stone, try to lift it themselves. A witch proposes the guarding of a herd of mares (159), and so forth.

2. *The donor greets and interrogates the hero* (D^2). This form may be considered as a weakened form of testing. Greeting and interrogation are also present in the forms mentioned above, but there they do not have the character of a test; rather they precede it. In the present case, however, direct testing is absent, and interrogation assumes the character of an indirect test. If the hero answers rudely he receives nothing, but if he responds politely he is rewarded with a steed, a sabre, and so on.

3. *A dying or deceased person requests the rendering of a service* (D^3). This form also sometimes takes on the character of a test. A cow requests the following: "Eat not of my meat, but gather up my bones, tie them in a kerchief, bury them in the garden, and forget me not, but water them each morning" (100). A similar request is made by the bull in tale No. 202.†† Another form of last wish is evident in tale No. 179. Here, a dying father instructs his sons to spend three nights beside his grave.

4. *A prisoner begs for his freedom* (D^4). The little brass peasant is held captive and asks to be freed (125). A devil sits in a tower and begs a soldier to free him (236). A jug fished out of water begs to be broken, i.e., the spirit within the jug asks for liberation (195).

† "Tri goda obsluživat' perevoz, ne berja voznagraždenija (71) . . ." (p. 49). This proposal is not found in tale 71; however, it does occur in tale 78 (= new no. 138). [L.A.W.]

†† The original reference (p. 50) is to tale 117. However, the request made in tale 118a (= new no. 202) would seem to fit better. [L.A.W.]

4*. The same as the preceding, accompanied by the preliminary imprisonment of the donor ($*D^4$). If, for example, as in tale No. 123, a forest spirit is caught, this deed cannot be considered an independent function: it merely sets the stage for the subsequent request of the captive.

5. *The hero is approached with a request for mercy* (D^5). This form might be considered as a subclass of the preceding one. It occurs either after capture or while the hero takes aim at an animal with the intention of killing it. The hero catches a pike which begs him to let it go (166); the hero aims at animals which beg to be spared (156).

6. *Disputants request a division of property* (D^6). Two giants ask that a staff and a broom be divided between them (185). Disputants do not always voice their request: the hero sometimes proposes a division on his own initiative (d^6). Beasts are incapable of sharing carrion; the hero divides it (162).

7. *Other requests* (D^7). Strictly speaking, requests as such constitute an independent class, while the individual types constitute subclasses; but in order to avoid an excessively cumbersome system of designation, one may arbitrarily consider all such varieties to be classes themselves. Having extracted the basic forms, the rest can be summarized. Mice ask to be fed (102); a thief asks the robbed person to carry the stolen goods for him (238). Next is a case which can immediately be assigned to two classes: A little vixen is caught; she begs, "Don't kill me (a request for mercy, D^5), fry me a hen with a little butter, as juicy as possible" (second request, D^7). Since imprisonment preceded this request, the designation for the complete happening is $*D_7^5$. An example of a different character, which also involves a suppliant's being threatened or caught up in a helpless situation is: the hero steals the clothes of a female bather who begs him to return them (219).† Sometimes a helpless situation

†". . . geroj poxiščaet u kupal'ščicy odeždu, ona prosit otdat' ee (131)" (p. 51). This does not occur in tale 131, but may be found, for example, in tales 125 and 71c (= new nos. 219 and 130). [L.A.W.]

simply occurs without any pronouncement of a request (fledglings become soaked in the rain, children torment a cat). In these instances the hero is presented with the possibility of rendering assistance. Objectively this amounts to a test, although subjectively the hero is not aware of it as such (d^7).

8. *A hostile creature attempts to destroy the hero* (D^8). A witch tries to place the hero in an oven (108). A witch attempts to behead heroes during the night (105). A host attempts to feed his guests to rats at night (216).† A magician tries to destroy the hero by leaving him alone on a mountain (243).

9. *A hostile creature engages the hero in combat* (D^9). A witch fights with the hero. Combat in a forest hut between the hero and various forest dwellers is encountered very often. Combat here has the character of a scuffle or brawl.

10. *The hero is shown a magical agent which is offered for exchange* (D^{10}). A robber shows a cudgel (215); merchants display wondrous objects (216); an old man displays a sword (270). They offer these things for exchange.

XIII. THE HERO REACTS TO THE ACTIONS OF THE FUTURE DONOR. (Definition: *the hero's reaction*. Designation: E.) In the majority of instances, the reaction is either positive or negative.

1. *The hero withstands (or does not withstand) a test* (E^1).
2. *The hero answers (or does not answer) a greeting* (E^2).
3. *He renders (or does not render) a service to a dead person* (E^3).
4. *He frees a captive* (E^4).
5. *He shows mercy to a suppliant* (E^5).
6. *He completes an apportionment and reconciles the*

† "Xozjain pytaetsja otdat' gostej noč'ju na s"edenie krysam (122)" (p. 51). This does not occur in tale 122, but may be found in 123 (= new no. 216). [L.A.W.]

disputants (E^6). The request of disputants (or simply an argument without a request) more often evokes a different reaction. The hero *deceives* the disputants, making them run, for example, after an arrow which he has shot into the distance; meanwhile, he himself seizes the disputed objects (E^{vi}).

7. *The hero performs some other service* (E^7). Sometimes these services correspond to requests; other times, they are done purely through the kindheartedness of the hero. A young girl feeds passing beggars (114). A special subclass might be made by forms of a religious nature. A hero burns a barrel of frankincense to the glory of God. To this group one instance of a prayer might also be relegated (115).

8. *The hero saves himself from an attempt on his life by employing the same tactics used by his adversary* (E^8). He puts the witch into the stove by making her show how to climb in (108). The heroes exchange clothes with the daughters of the witch in secret; she proceeds to kill them instead of the heroes (105). The magician himself remains on the mountain where he wanted to abandon the hero (243).

9. *The hero vanquishes (or does not vanquish) his adversary* (E^9).

10. *The hero agrees to an exchange, but immediately employs the magic power of the object exchanged against the barterer* (E^{10}). An old man offers to trade his magic sword to a cossack for a magic cask. The cossack makes the exchange, whereupon he orders the sword to cut off the old man's head, thus getting back the cask also (270).

XIV. THE HERO ACQUIRES THE USE OF A MAGICAL AGENT. (Definition: *provision or receipt of a magical agent.* Designation: F.)

The following things are capable of serving as magical agents: (1) animals (a horse, an eagle, etc.); (2) objects out of which magical helpers appear (a flintstone containing a steed, a ring containing young men); (3) objects possessing a magical property, such as cudgels, swords, guslas, balls, and many others; (4) qualities or capacities which are directly given, such as the power of transformation into animals, etc. All of these objects of transmission we shall conditionally term "magical agents."[4] The forms by which they are transmitted are the following:

1. *The agent is directly transferred* (F^1). Such acts of transference very often have the character of a reward: an old man presents a horse as a gift; forest animals offer their offspring, etc. Sometimes the hero, instead of receiving a certain animal directly for his own use, obtains the power of turning himself into it (for details see Chapter VI). Some tales end with the moment of reward. In these instances the gift amounts to something of a certain material value and is not a magical agent (f^1). If a hero's reaction is negative, then the transference may not occur (F neg.), or is replaced by cruel retribution. The hero is devoured, frozen, has strips cut out of his back, is thrown under a stone, etc. (F contr.).
2. *The agent is pointed out* (F^2). An old woman indicates an oak tree under which lies a flying ship (144).† An old man points out a peasant from whom a magic steed may be obtained (138).
3. *The agent is prepared* (F^3). "The magician went out on the shore, drew a boat in the sand and said: 'Well, brothers, do you see this boat?' 'We see it.' 'Get into it.' " (138).
4. *The agent is sold and purchased* (F^4). The hero buys a magic hen (197);†† he buys a magic dog and cat (190), etc. The intermediate form between purchase and preparation is "preparation on order"; the hero places an order for a chain to be made by a blacksmith (105). (The designation for this instance: F_4^3).
5. *The agent falls into the hands of the hero by chance (is found by him)* (F^5). Iván sees a horse in the field and

† "Staruxa ukazyvaet dub, pod kotorym naxoditsja letučij korabl' (83)" (p. 53). In the given tale, it is not an old woman, but an old man (*starik*) who indicates the tree. [L.A.W.]

†† "Geroj pokupaet volšebnuju kuru (114)" (p. 54). The hero buys a hen in tale 115 (= new no. 197) but not in tale 114. In the latter he is told how to get a magic duck. [L.A.W.]

mounts him (132); he comes upon a tree bearing magic apples (192).

6. *The agent suddenly appears of its own accord* (F^{6}). A staircase suddenly appears, leading up a mountainside (156). Agents sprouting out of the ground constitute a special form of independent appearance (F^{vi}), and they may be magical bushes (100, 101), twigs, a dog and a horse (201), or a dwarf.

7. *The agent is eaten or drunk* (F^{7}). This is not, strictly speaking, a form of transference, although it may be coordinated, conditionally, with the cases cited. Three beverages provide the drinker with unusual strength (125); the eating of a bird's giblets endows heroes with various magical qualities (195).

8. *The agent is seized* (F^{8}). The hero steals a horse from a witch (159); he seizes the disputed objects (197). The application of magical agents against the person who exchanged them and the taking back of objects which had been given may also be considered a special form of seizure.

9. *Various characters place themselves at the disposal of the hero* (F^{9}). An animal, for example, may either present its offspring or offer its services to the hero, making, as it were, a present of itself. Let us compare the following instances: A steed is not always presented directly, or in a flintstone. Sometimes the donor simply informs the hero of an incantation formula with which the hero may invoke the steed to appear. In the latter instance, Iván is not actually given anything: he only receives the right to a helper. We have the same situation when the suppliant offers Iván the right to make use of him: the pike informs Iván of a formula by which he may call it forth ("Say only: 'by the pike's command . . .' "). If, finally, the formula also is omitted, and the animal simply promises, "Sometime I'll be of use to you," then we still have before us a moment in which the hero receives the aid of a magical agent in the form of an animal. Later on it will become Iván's helper (f^{9}). It often happens that various magical creatures, without any warning, suddenly appear or are met on the way and offer

their services and are accepted as helpers (F_9^6). Most often these are heroes with extraordinary attributes, or characters possessing various magical qualities (Overeater, Overdrinker, Crackling Frost).

Here, before continuing with the further registration of functions, the following question may be raised: in what combination does one encounter the types of elements D (preparation for transmission), and F (transmission itself)?[5] One need only state that, in the face of a negative reaction on the part of the hero, one encounters only F neg. (the transmission does not take place), or F contr. (the unfortunate hero is severely punished). Under the condition of the hero's positive reaction, however, one encounters the combinations shown in Figure 1.

One can see from this scheme that the connections are exceptionally varied, and that consequently a wide range of substitution of certain variations for others can be ascertained on the whole. Yet if one examines this scheme more carefully, one immediately becomes aware of the absence of several connections. This absence is in part explained by the insufficiency of material, but certain combinations would not prove logical. Therefore we conclude that there exist *types* of connections. If one proceeds to determine types from the forms of transmission of a magical agent, one can isolate two types of connections:

1. The seizure of a magical agent, linked with an attempt to destroy the hero (roast, etc.), with a request for apportionment, or with a proposal for an exchange.
2. All other forms of transmission and receipt, linked with all other preparatory forms. The request for apportionment belongs to the second type if the division is actually accomplished, but to the first if the disputants are deceived. Further, it is possible to observe that a find, a purchase, and a sudden independent appearance of a magical agent or helper are most often encountered without the slightest preparation. These are rudimentary forms. But if they nevertheless *are* prepared, then this occurs in forms of the second type, and not the first.

In connection with this, one might touch upon the question of

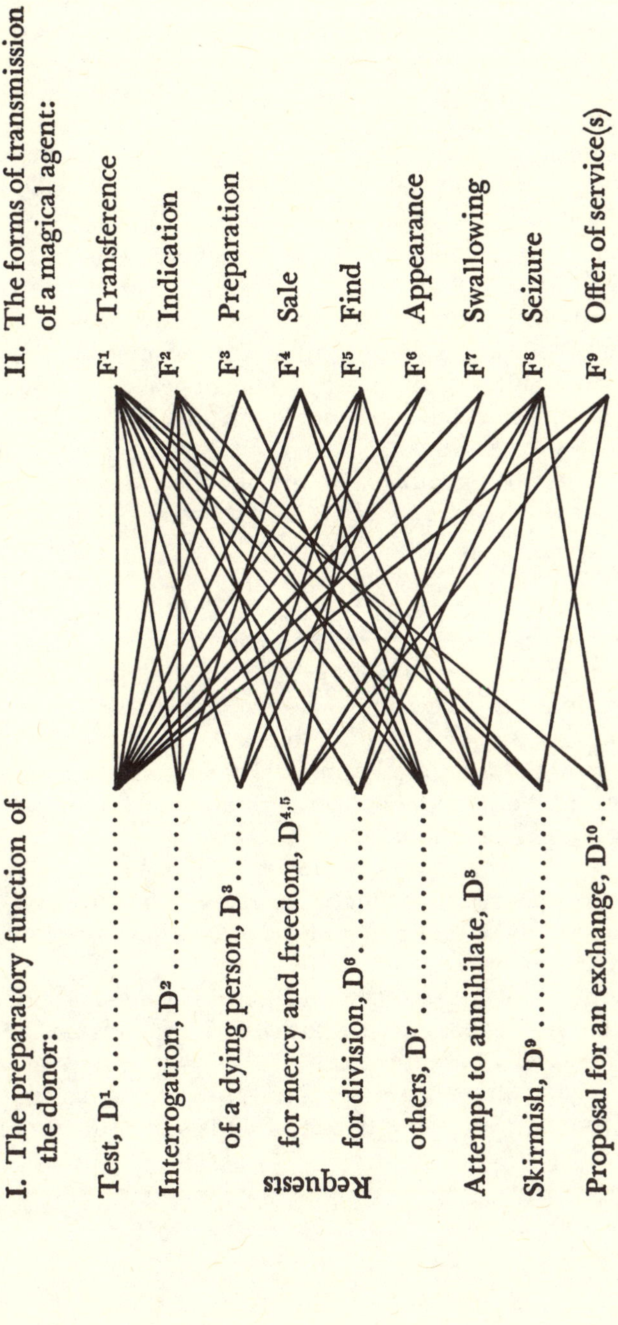
I. The preparatory function of the donor:
Test, D^1
Interrogation, D^2
Requests
of a dying person, D^3
for mercy and freedom, $D^{4,5}$
for division, D^6
others, D^7
Attempt to annihilate, D^8
Skirmish, D^9
Proposal for an exchange, D^{10}
II. The forms of transmission of a magical agent:
F^1 Transference
F^2 Indication
F^3 Preparation
F^4 Sale
F^5 Find
F^6 Appearance
F^7 Swallowing
F^8 Seizure
F^9 Offer of service(s)

FIGURE 1

the character of donors. The second type most often presents friendly donors (with the exception of those who surrender a magical agent unwillingly or after a fight), whereas the first type exhibits unfriendly (or, at any rate, deceived) donors. These are not donors in the true sense of the word, but personages who unwillingly furnish the hero with something. Within the forms of each type, all combinations are possible and logical, whether actually present or not. Thus, for example, either an exacting or a grateful donor is capable of giving, revealing, selling, or preparing an agent, or he may let the hero find the agent, etc. On the other hand, an agent in the possession of a deceived donor can only be stolen or taken by force. Combinations outside of these types are illogical. Thus, for example, it is not logical if a hero, after performing a difficult task for a witch, steals a colt from her. This does not mean that such combinations do not exist in the tale. They do exist, but in these instances the storyteller is obliged to give additional motivation for the actions of his heroes. Here is another model of an illogical connection which is clearly motivated: Iván fights with an old man. During the struggle the old man *inadvertently* permits Iván to drink some strength-giving water. This "inadvertence" becomes understandable when one compares this incident with those tales in which a beverage is given by a grateful or a generally friendly donor. In this manner we see that the lack of logic in the connection is not a stumbling block to the storyteller.

If one were to follow a purely empirical approach, one would have to confirm the interchangeability of all the various forms of elements D and F in relation to each other.

Below are several concrete examples of connection:

Type II: $D^1E^1F^1$. A witch forces the hero to take a herd of mares to pasture. A second task follows, the hero accomplishes it, and receives a horse (160).

$D^2E^2F^2$. An old man interrogates the hero. He answers rudely and receives nothing. Later, he returns and responds politely, whereupon he receives a horse (155).

$D^3E^3F^1$. A dying father requests his sons to spend three nights beside his grave. The youngest son fulfills the request and receives a horse (180).†

† The original textual reference (p. 57) is tale 195; this is incorrect. The connection described may be found in tale 105b (= new no. 180). [L.A.W.]

$D^8E^8F^{vi}$. A young bull asks the tsar's children to kill him, burn him, and plant his ashes in three beds. The hero does these things. From one bed an apple tree sprouts forth; from the second a dog; and from the third a horse (201).†

$D^1E^1F^5$. Brothers find a large stone. "Can't it be moved?" (trial without a tester). The elder brothers cannot move it. The youngest moves the stone, revealing below it a vault, and in the vault Iván finds three horses (137).

This list could be continued *ad libitum*. It is important only to note that in similar situations other magical gifts besides horses are presented. The examples given here with steeds were selected for the purpose of more sharply outlining a morphological kinship.

Type I: $D^6E^{vi}F^8$. Three disputants request the apportionment of magical objects. The hero instructs them to chase after one another, and in the meanwhile, he seizes the objects (a cap, a rug, boots).

$D^8E^8F^8$. Heroes fall into the hands of a witch. At night she plans to behead them. They put her daughters in their place and run away, the youngest brother making off with a magic kerchief (105).††

$D^{10}E^{10}F^8$. Šmat-Rázum, an invisible spirit, serves the hero. Three merchants offer a little chest (a garden), an axe (a boat), and a horn (an army) in exchange for the spirit. The hero agrees to the barter but later calls his helper back to him.

We observe that the substitution of certain aspects by others, within the confines of each type, is practiced on a large scale. Another question is whether or not certain *objects* of transmission are connected to certain *forms* of transmission (i.e., is not a horse always given, whereas a flying carpet is always seized, etc.)? Although our examination pertains solely to functions per se, we can indicate (without proofs) that no such norm exists. A

† "Byčok prosit carskix detej ego zarezat', sžeč', i pepel posejat' na trex grjadkax. Geroj èto vypolnjaet. Iz odnoj grjadki vyrostaet jablonja, iz drugoj—sobaka, iz tret'ej—kon' (118)" (p. 57). This happens in tale 117 (= new no. 201), not in 118. In tale 118 the bull says, "Kill me and eat me, but gather up my bones and strike them; from them a little old man will come forth . . ." [L.A.W.]

†† "Geroi popadajut k jage. Ona xočet noč'ju otrubit' im golovy. Oni podsovyvajut ej ee dočerej. Brat'ja begut, mladšij poxiščaet volšebnyj platoček (61)" (p. 58). This situation does not occur in tale 61, but it may be found (with slight variations) in tale 60 (= new no. 105). [L.A.W.]

horse, which is usually given, is seized in tale No. 159.† On the other hand, a magic kerchief, which affords rescue from pursuit, and which is usually seized, is instead given as a gift to the hero in tale No. 159 and others.†† A flying ship may be prepared, or pointed out, or given as a gift, etc.

Let us return to the enumeration of the functions of dramatis personae. The employment of a magical agent follows its receipt by the hero; or, if the agent received is a living creature, its help is directly put to use on the command of the hero. With this the hero outwardly loses all significance; he himself does nothing, while his helper accomplishes everything. The morphological significance of the hero is nevertheless very great, since his intentions create the axis of the narrative. These intentions appear in the form of various commands which the hero gives to his helpers. At this point a more exact definition of the hero can be given than was done before. The hero of a fairy tale is that character who either directly suffers from the action of the villain in the complication (the one who senses some kind of lack), or who agrees to liquidate the misfortune or lack of another person. In the course of the action the hero is the person who is supplied with a magical agent (a magical helper), and who makes use of it or is served by it.

XV. THE HERO IS TRANSFERRED, DELIVERED, OR LED TO THE WHEREABOUTS OF AN OBJECT OF SEARCH. (Definition: *spatial transference between two kingdoms, guidance*. Designation: G.)

Generally the object of search is located in "another" or "different" kingdom. This kingdom may lie far away horizontally, or else very high up or deep down vertically. The means of unification may be identical in all cases, but specific forms do exist for great heights and depths.

† "Kon', kotoryj čašče vsego daetsja, v skazke No. 95 poxiščaetsja" (p. 58). On the contrary, in tale 95 the witch lets Iván choose whichever foal he wants from the stable. A tale in which Iván steals a foal would be 94 (= new no. 159). [L.A.W.]

†† "Naoborot, volšebnyj platoček . . . v skazke No. 94 i dr. daritsja" (p. 58). To be more specific, in tale 94 Mar'ja Morevna first steals the magic kerchief from Koščéj, and then passes it on to Iván. [L.A.W.]

1. *The hero flies through the air* (G^1): on a steed (171); on a bird (219); † in the form of a bird (162); on board a flying ship (138); on a flying carpet (192); on the back of a giant or a spirit (212); †† in the carriage of a devil (154); and so forth. Flight on a bird is sometimes accompanied by a detail: it is necessary to feed the bird on the journey, so the hero brings along an ox, etc.
2. *He travels on the ground or on water* (G^2): on the back of a horse or wolf (168); on board a ship (247); a handless person carries a legless one (198); a cat swims a river on the back of a dog (190).
3. *He is led* (G^3). A ball of thread shows the way (234); a fox leads the hero to the princess (163).
4. *The route is shown to him* (G^4). A hedgehog points out the way to a kidnapped brother (113).
5. *He makes use of stationary means of communication* (G^5). He climbs a stairway (156); he finds an underground passageway and makes use of it (141); he walks across the back of an enormous pike, as across a bridge (156); he descends by means of leather straps, etc.
6. *He follows bloody tracks* (G^6). The hero defeats the inhabitant of a forest hut who runs away, hiding himself under a stone. Following his tracks Iván finds the entrance into another kingdom.

This exhausts the forms of transference of the hero. It should be noted that "delivery," as a function in itself, is sometimes absent: the hero simply walks to the place (i.e., function G amounts to a natural continuation of function ↑). In such a case function G is not singled out.

XVI. THE HERO AND THE VILLAIN JOIN IN DIRECT COMBAT. (Definition: *struggle.* Designation: H.)

This form needs to be distinguished from the struggle (fight) with a hostile donor. These two forms can be distinguished by their results. If the hero obtains an agent, for the purpose of

† ". . . na ptice (121) . . ." (p. 59). This does not occur in tale 121, but may be found, for example, in tale 125 (= new no. 219). [L.A.W.]

†† ". . . na spine velikana ili duxa (121) . . ." (p. 59). This does not happen in tale 121, but occurs, for example, in tale 122 (= new no. 212). [L.A.W.]

further searching, as the result of an unfriendly encounter, this would be element D. If, on the other hand, the hero receives through victory the very object of his quest, we have situation H.

1. *They fight in an open field* (H^1). Here, first of all, belong fights with dragons or with Čúdo-Júdo, etc. (125), and also battles with an enemy army or a knight, etc. (212).
2. *They engage in a competition* (H^2). In humorous tales the fight itself sometimes does not occur. After a squabble (often completely analogous to the squabble that precedes an out-and-out-fight), the hero and the villain engage in a competition. The hero wins with the help of cleverness: a gypsy puts a dragon to flight by squeezing a piece of cheese as though it were a stone, by pretending that a blow to the back of the head was merely a whistle, etc. (149).†
3. *They play cards* (H^3). The hero and a dragon (a devil) play cards (192, 153).
4. Tale No. 93 presents a special form: a she-dragon†† proposes the following to the hero: "Let Prince Iván get on the scales with me; who will outweigh the other?"[6] (H^4).

XVII. THE HERO IS BRANDED. (Definition: *branding, marking*. Designation: J.)

1. *A brand is applied to the body* (J^1). The hero receives a wound during the skirmish. A princess awakens him before the fight by making a small wound in his cheek with a knife (125). A princess brands the hero on the forehead with a signet ring (195); she kisses him, leaving a burning star on his forehead.
2. *The hero receives a ring or a towel* (J^2). We have a combination of two forms if the hero is wounded in battle and the wound is bound with the kerchief of either a princess or a king.

† The original reference here (p. 60) is to tale 85. However, the trickery described takes place in tale 86 (= new no. 149). [L.A.W.]

†† Cf. footnote on page 68. [L.A.W.]

XVIII. THE VILLAIN IS DEFEATED. (Definition: *victory.* Designation: I.)

1. *The villain is beaten in open combat* (I^1).
2. *He is defeated in a contest* (I^2).
3. *He loses at cards* (I^3).
4. *He loses on being weighed* (I^4).
5. *He is killed without a preliminary fight* (I^5). A dragon is killed while asleep (141). Zmiulán hides in the hollow of a tree; he is killed (164).
6. *He is banished directly* (I^6). A princess, possessed by a devil, places a sacred image around her neck: "The evil power flew away in a puff of smoke" (115).

Victory is also encountered in a negative form. If two or three heroes have gone out to do battle, one of them (a general) hides, while the other is victorious (designation: $*I^1$).

XIX. THE INITIAL MISFORTUNE OR LACK IS LIQUIDATED. (Designation: K.) This function, together with villainy (A), constitutes a pair. The narrative reaches its peak in this function.

1. *The object of a search is seized by the use of force or cleverness* (K^1). Here heroes sometimes employ the same means adopted by villains for the initial seizure. Iván's steed turns into a beggar who goes seeking alms. The princess gives them. Iván runs out of the bushes; they seize her and carry her away (185).

1a. Sometimes the capture is accomplished by two personages, one of whom orders the other to perform the actual business of catching (K^1). A horse steps on a crawfish and orders it to bring him a bridal dress. A cat catches a mouse and orders it to fetch a little ring (190).

2. *The object of search is obtained by several personages at once, through a rapid interchange of their actions* (K^2).

The distribution of action is evoked by a series of consecutive failures or attempts on the part of the abducted person to escape. The seven Semjóns obtain a princess: the thief kidnaps her, but she flies away in the form of a swan; the archer shoots her down, and another one, in place of a dog, retrieves her from the water, etc. (145). Similarly, the egg containing Koščéj's death is obtained. A hare, a duck, and a fish run away, fly away, and swim away with the egg. A wolf, a raven, and a fish obtain it (156).

3. *The object of search is obtained with the help of enticements* (K^3). This form, in many instances, is quite close in nature to K^1. The hero lures the princess on board a ship with the aid of golden objects and carries her away (242). A special subclass might be made out of an enticement in the form of a proposal for an exchange. A blinded girl embroiders a wonderful crown and sends it to her villainous servant girl. In exchange for the crown the latter returns the eyes, which are thus retrieved.

4. *The object of a quest is obtained as the direct result of preceding actions* (K^4). If, for example, Iván kills a dragon and later marries the princess whom he has freed, there is no obtaining as a special act; rather, there is obtaining as a function, as a stage in the development of the plot. The princess is neither seized nor abducted, but she is nevertheless "obtained." She is obtained as the result of combat. Obtaining in these cases is a logical element. It may also be accomplished as a result of acts other than battles. Thus Iván can *find* a princess as the result of making a guided journey.

5. *The object of search is obtained instantly through the use of a magical agent* (K^5). Two young men (appearing out of a magical book) deliver a golden-horned stag with the speed of a whirlwind (212).

6. *The use of a magical agent overcomes poverty* (K^6). A magic duck lays golden eggs (195). The magic tablecloth which sets itself and the horse that scatters gold both belong here (186). Another form of the self-setting tablecloth appears in the image of a pike: "By the pike's command and God's blessing let the table be set and the dinner ready!" (167).

7. *The object of search is caught* (K^7). This form is typical for agrarian pillage. The hero catches a mare

which was stealing hay (105). He captures the crane which was stealing peas (187).

8. *The spell on a person is broken* (K^8). This form is typical for A^{11} (enchantment). The breaking of a spell takes place either by burning the hide or by means of a formula: "Be a girl once again!"

9. *A slain person is revived* (K^9). A hairpin or a dead tooth is removed from a head (210, 202). The hero is sprinkled with deadening and life-giving waters.

9a. Just as in the case of reverse capture one animal forces another to act, here also a wolf catches a raven and forces its mother to bring some deadening water and some life-giving water (168). This means of revival, preceded by the obtaining of water, may be singled out as a special subclass (K^{1x}).[7]

10. *A captive is freed* (K^{10}). A horse breaks open the doors of a dungeon and frees Iván (185). This form, morphologically speaking, has nothing in common, for example, with the freeing of a forest spirit, since in the latter case a basis for gratitude and for the giving of a magical agent is created. Here initial misfortune is done away with. Tale No. 259 evidences a special form of liberation: here, the king of the sea always drags his prisoner out onto the shore at midnight. The hero beseeches the sun to free him. The sun is late on two occasions. On the third occasion "the sun shone forth its rays and the king of the sea could no longer drag him back into bondage."

11. The receipt of an object of search is sometimes accomplished by means of the same forms as the receipt of a magical agent (i.e., it is given as a gift, its location is indicated, it is purchased, etc.). Designation of these occurrences: KF^1, direct transmission; KF^2, indication; etc., as above.

XX. THE HERO RETURNS. (Definition: *return*. Designation: ↓.)

A return is generally accomplished by means of the same forms as an arrival. However, there is no need of attaching a special function to follow a return, since returning already implies a surmounting of space. This is not always true in the case of a departure. Following a departure, an agent is given (a horse, eagle, etc.) and then flying or other forms of travel occur, whereas a return takes place immediately and, for the most part, in the same forms as an arrival. Sometimes return has the nature of fleeing.

XXI. THE HERO IS PURSUED. (Definition: *pursuit, chase*. Designation: Pr.)

1. *The pursuer flies after the hero* (Pr^1). A dragon catches up to Iván (160); a witch flies after a boy (105); † geese fly after a girl (113).
2. *He demands the guilty person* (Pr^2). This form is also mostly linked with actual flight through the air: The father of a dragon dispatches a flying boat. From the boat they shout, "[we want] the guilty one, the guilty one!" (125).
3. *He pursues the hero, rapidly transforming himself into various animals, etc.* (Pr^3). This form at several stages is also connected with flight: a magician pursues the hero in the forms of a wolf, a pike, a man, and a rooster (249).
4. *Pursuers (dragons' wives, etc.) turn into alluring objects and place themselves in the path of the hero* (Pr^4). "I'll run ahead and make the day hot for him, and I shall turn myself into a green meadow. In this green meadow I'll change into a well, and in this well there shall swim a silver goblet . . . here they'll be torn asunder like poppy seeds" (136). She-dragons change into gardens, pillows, wells, etc. The tale does not inform us, however, as to how they manage to get ahead of the hero.
5. *The pursuer tries to devour the hero* (Pr^5). A she-dragon turns into a maiden, seduces the hero, and then changes into a lioness that wants to devour Iván (155).

† ". . . ved'ma letit za mal'čikom (60)" (p. 64). In the text cited, the witch flies after a group of bold youths (*molodcy*). [L.A.W.]

A dragon mother opens her jaws from the sky to the earth (138).†

6. *The pursuer attempts to kill the hero* (Pr^6). He tries to pound a dead tooth into his head (202).

7. *He tries to gnaw through a tree in which the hero is taking refuge* (Pr^7).

XXII. RESCUE OF THE HERO FROM PURSUIT. (Definition: *rescue*. Designation: Rs.)

1. *He is carried away through the air* (sometimes he is saved by lightning-fast fleeing) (Rs^1). The hero flies away on a horse (160), on geese (108).

2. *The hero flees, placing obstacles in the path of his pursuer* (Rs^2). He throws a brush, a comb, a towel. They turn into mountains, forests, lakes. Similarly, Vertogór (Mountain-Turner) and Vertodúb (Oak-Turner) tear up mountains and oak trees, placing them in the path of the she-dragon (93).††

3. *The hero, while in flight, changes into objects which make him unrecognizable* (Rs^3). A princess turns herself and the prince into a well and dipper, a church and priest (219).

4. *The hero hides himself during his flight* (Rs^4). A river, an apple tree, and a stove hide a maiden (113).

5. *The hero is hidden by blacksmiths* (Rs^5). A she-dragon demands the guilty person. Iván has hidden with blacksmiths, and they seize the dragon by the tongue and beat her with their hammers (136). An incident in tale No. 153 undoubtedly is related to this form: devils are placed in a knapsack by a soldier, are carried to a smithy and beaten with heavy hammers.

6. *The hero saves himself while in flight by means of rapid transformations into animals, stones, etc.* (Rs^6). The hero flees in the form of a horse, a ruff, a ring, a seed, a falcon (249). The actual transformation is essential to this form. Flight may sometimes be omitted; such forms may be considered as a special subclass. A maiden

† "Zmeixa-mat' otkryvaet past' ot neba do zemli (92)" (p. 65). This does not occur in tale 92, but may be found in tale 78 (= new no. 138). [L.A.W.]

†† Cf. the footnote on p. 68. [L.A.W.]

is killed and a garden springs forth from her remains. The garden is cut down, it turns to stone, etc. (127).

7. *He avoids the temptations of transformed she-dragons* (Rs[7]). Iván hacks at the garden, the well, and so forth; blood flows from them (137).

8. *He does not allow himself to be devoured* (Rs[8]). Iván jumps his horse over the she-dragon's jaws. He recognizes the lioness as the she-dragon and kills her (155).†

9. *He is saved from an attempt on his life* (Rs[9]). Animals extract the dead tooth from his head in the nick of time.

10. *He jumps to another tree* (Rs[10]).

A great many tales end on the note of rescue from pursuit. The hero arrives home and then, if he has obtained a girl, marries her, etc. Nevertheless, this is far from always being the case. A tale may have another misfortune in store for the hero: a villain may appear once again, may seize whatever Iván has obtained, may kill Iván, etc. In a word, an initial villainy is repeated, sometimes in the same forms as in the beginning, and sometimes in other forms which are new for a given tale. With this a new story commences. There are no specific forms of repeated villainies (i.e., we again have abduction, enchantment, murder, etc.), but there are specific villains connected with the new misfortune. They are Iván's elder brothers. Shortly after his arrival home they steal his prize and sometimes kill even him. If they permit him to remain alive then, in order to instigate a new search, it is necessary once more to place a great spatial barrier between the hero and the object being sought. This is accomplished by their throwing him into a chasm (into a pit, a subterranean kingdom, or sometimes into the sea), into which he may sometimes fall for three whole days. Then everything begins anew: i.e., again an accidental meeting with a donor; a successfully completed ordeal or service rendered, etc.; a receipt of a magical agent and its employment to return the hero home to

† "On uznaet v l'vice zmeixu i ubivaet ee (92)" (p. 66). However, in the tale referred to ("The Two Iváns, Soldier's Sons"; new no. 155), the first Iván does not kill the lioness, he only *threatens* to do so if she does not regurgitate his brother, the second Iván. She spits up the dead brother, he is revived, and then the lioness is pardoned. Cf. the detailed analysis of this tale (Appendix II, no. 8), where the same misinterpretation appears again, resulting in some confusion. [L.A.W.]

his own kingdom. From this moment on the development is different from that in the beginning of the tale; we shall consider it below.

This phenomenon attests to the fact that many tales are composed of two *series* of functions which may be labelled "moves" (*xodý*). A new villainous act creates a new "move," and in this manner, sometimes a whole series of tales combine into a single tale. Nevertheless, the process of development which will be described below does constitute the continuation of a given tale, although it also creates a new move. In connection with this, one must eventually ask how to distinguish the number of tales in each text.

VIII$_{bis}$. *Iván's brothers steal his prize (and throw him into a chasm.)*

Villainy has already been designated as A. If the brothers kidnap Iván's bride, the designation for this act would be A^1. If they steal a magical agent, then the designation is A^2. Abduction accompanied by murder is termed A_{14}^1. Forms connected with the hero's being thrown into a chasm shall be designated as $*A^1$, $*A^2$, $*A_{14}^2$, and so forth.

X–XI$_{bis}$. *The hero once more sets out in search of something* (C↑) (see X–XI).

This element is sometimes omitted here. Iván wanders about and weeps, as though not thinking about returning. Element B (dispatch) is also always absent in these instances, since there is no reason for dispatching Iván, as he is the one from whom the bride has been kidnapped.

XII$_{bis}$. *The hero once again is the subject of actions leading to the receipt of a magical agent* (D) (see XII).

XIII$_{bis}$. *The hero again reacts to the actions of the future donor* (E) (see XIII).

XIV$_{bis}$. *A new magical agent is placed at the hero's disposal* (F) (see XIV).

XV$_{bis}$. *The hero is brought or transported to the location of the object of the quest* (G) (see XV). In this case he reaches *home.*

From this point onward, the development of the narrative proceeds differently, and the tale gives new functions.

XXIII. THE HERO, UNRECOGNIZED, ARRIVES HOME OR IN ANOTHER COUNTRY. (Definition: *unrecognized arrival.* Designation: o.)

Here, two classes are distinguishable: (1) arrival *home,* in which the hero stays with some sort of artisan (goldsmith, tailor, shoemaker, etc.), serving as an apprentice; (2) he arrives at the court of some *king,* and serves either as a cook or a groom. At the same time it is sometimes necessary to designate simple arrival as well.

XXIV. A FALSE HERO PRESENTS UNFOUNDED CLAIMS. (Definition: *unfounded claims.* Designation: L.)

If the hero arrives home, the false claims are presented by his brothers. If he is serving in another kingdom, a general, a water-carrier, or others present them. The brothers pose as capturers of the prize; the general poses as the conqueror of a dragon. These two forms can be considered special classes.

XXV. A DIFFICULT TASK IS PROPOSED TO THE HERO. (Definition: *difficult task.* Designation: M.)

This is one of the tale's favorite elements. Tasks are also assigned outside the connections just described, but these connections will be dealt with somewhat later. At the moment, let us take up the matter of the tasks per se. These tasks are so varied that each would need a special designation. However, there is no need at present to go into these details. Since no exact distribution will be made, we shall enumerate all instances present in our material, with an approximate arrangement into groups:

Ordeal by food and drink: to eat a certain number of oxen or wagonloads of bread; to drink a great deal of beer (137, 138, 144).

Ordeal by fire: to bathe in a red-hot iron bathhouse. This form is always connected with the previous ordeal (137, 138, 144). A separate form: a bath in boiling water (169).

Riddle guessing and similar ordeals: to pose an unsolvable riddle (239); to recount and interpret a dream (241); to explain the meaning of the ravens' croaking at the tsar's window, and to drive them away (247); to find out (to guess) the distinctive marks of a tsar's daughter (238).

Ordeal of choice: to select sought-after persons among twelve identical girls (or boys) (219, 227, 249).

Hide and seek: to hide oneself so that discovery is impossible (236).

To kiss the princess in a window (180, 182).†

To jump up on top of the gates (101).

Test of strength, adroitness, fortitude: a princess chokes Iván at night or squeezes his hand (198, 136); the task of picking up the heads of a decapitated dragon (171), of breaking in a horse (198), of milking a herd of wild mares (170),†† of defeating an amazon (202), or a rival (167), is given to the hero.

Test of endurance: to spend seven years in the tin kingdom (270).

Tasks of supply and manufacture: to supply a medicine (123); to obtain a wedding dress, a ring, shoes (132, 139, 156, 169); to deliver the hair of the king of the sea (240); to deliver a flying boat (144); to deliver life-giving water (144); to supply a troop of soldiers (144); to obtain seventy-seven mares (170);††† to build a palace during one night (190), a bridge leading to it (216);‡ to bring "the mate to my unknown one to make a pair," (240).‡‡

As tasks of manufacture: to sew shirts (104, 267); to bake bread (267); as the third task in this case, the tsar asks who dances better.

Other tasks: to pick berries from a certain bush or tree (100, 101); to cross a pit on a pole (137); to find someone "whose candle will light by itself" (195).

The method of differentiation of these tasks from other highly similar elements will be outlined in the chapter on assimilations.

† The texts cited (p. 69) are nos. 105 and 106. More specifically, 105 should be 105b (= new no. 180). [L.A.W.]

†† The text cited (p. 69) is 103. More accurately, it should be 103b (= new no. 170). [L.A.W.]

††† The text cited (p. 69) is 103. More specifically, it should be 103b (= new no. 170). [L.A.W.]

‡ ". . . most k nemu (121)" (p. 69). However, the task of building a bridge to the palace does not occur in tale 121, but may be found in tale 123 (= new no. 216). [L.A.W.]

‡‡ "Prinesti ' k moemu neznaemomu pod paru ' (113)" (p. 69). Such a task is not set in tale 113, but does occur in tale 133 (= new no. 240). What is involved here is that a princess requires Iván to produce the exact mate to some object (e.g., an embroidered slipper) without knowing beforehand what the object is. [L.A.W.]

XXVI. THE TASK IS RESOLVED. (Definition: *solution.* Designation: N.)

Forms of solution correspond exactly, of course, to the forms of tasks. Certain tasks are completed before they are set, or before the time required by the person assigning the task. Thus the hero finds out the princess' distinctive marks before he is requested to do so. Preliminary solutions of this type shall be designated by the sign *N.

XXVII. THE HERO IS RECOGNIZED. (Definition: *recognition.* Designation: Q.)

He is recognized by a mark, a brand (a wound, a star marking), or by a thing given to him (a ring, towel). In this case, recognition serves as a function corresponding to branding and marking. The hero is also recognized by his accomplishment of a difficult task (this is almost always preceded by an unrecognized arrival). Finally, the hero may be recognized immediately after a long period of separation. In the latter case, parents and children, brothers and sisters, etc., may recognize one another.

XXVIII. THE FALSE HERO OR VILLAIN IS EXPOSED. (Definition: *exposure.* Designation: Ex.)

This function is, in most cases, connected with the one preceding. Sometimes it is the result of an uncompleted task (the false hero cannot lift the dragon's heads). Most often it is presented in the form of a story ("Here the princess told everything as it was"). Sometimes all the events are recounted from the very beginning in the form of a tale. The villain is among the listeners, and he gives himself away by expressions of disapproval (197). Sometimes a song is sung telling of what has occurred and exposing the villain (244). Other unique forms of exposure also occur (258).

XXIX. THE HERO IS GIVEN A NEW APPEARANCE. (Definition: *transfiguration.* Designation: T.)

1. *A new appearance is directly effected by means of the magical action of a helper* (T^1). The hero passes through the ears of a horse (or cow) and receives a new, handsome appearance.

2. *The hero builds a marvelous palace* (T^2). He resides in the palace himself as the prince. A maiden suddenly awakens during the night in a marvelous palace (127). Although the hero is not always transformed in these instances, he nevertheless does undergo a change in personal appearance.

3. *The hero puts on new garments* (T^3). A girl puts on a (magical?) dress and ornaments and suddenly is endowed with a radiant beauty at which everyone marvels (234).

4. *Rationalized and humorous forms* (T^4). These forms are partly explained by those preceding (as their transformations), and, in part, must be studied and explained in connection with the study of tale-anecdotes, whence they originate. Actual changes of appearance do not take place in these cases, but a new appearance is achieved by deception. For example, a fox leads Kúzin'ka to a king saying that Kúzin'ka fell into a ditch and requests clothes. The fox is given royal garments. Kúzin'ka appears in the royal attire and is taken for a tsar's son. All similar instances may be formulated in the following manner: false evidence of wealth and beauty is accepted as true evidence.

XXX. THE VILLAIN IS PUNISHED. (Definition: *punishment.* Designation. U.)

The villain is shot, banished, tied to the tail of a horse, commits suicide, and so forth. In parallel with this we sometimes have a magnanimous pardon (U neg.). Usually only the villain of the second move and the false hero are punished, while the first villain is punished only in those cases in which a battle and pursuit are absent from the story. Otherwise, he is killed in battle or perishes during the pursuit (a witch bursts in an attempt to drink up the sea, etc.).

XXXI. THE HERO IS MARRIED AND ASCENDS THE THRONE. (Definition: *wedding.* Designation: W.)

1. A bride and a kingdom are awarded at once, or the hero receives half the kingdom at first, and the whole kingdom upon the death of the parents (W^{*}_{*}).

2. Sometimes the hero simply marries without obtaining a throne, since his bride is not a princess (W^*).
3. Sometimes, on the contrary, only accession to the throne is mentioned (W_*).
4. If a new act of villainy interrupts a tale shortly before a wedding, then the first move ends with a betrothal, or a promise of marriage (w^1).
5. In contrast to the preceding case, a married hero loses his wife; the marriage is resumed as the result of a quest (designation for a resumed marriage: w^2).
6. The hero sometimes receives a monetary reward or some other form of compensation in place of the princess' hand (w^o).

At this point the tale draws to a close. It should also be stated that there are several actions of tale heroes in individual cases which do not conform to, nor are defined by, any of the functions already mentioned. Such cases are rare. They are either forms which cannot be understood without comparative material, or they are forms transferred from tales of other classes (anecdotes, legends, etc.). We define these as unclear elements and designate them with the sign X.

Just what are the conclusions that may be drawn from the foregoing observations? First of all, a few *general* inferences. We observe that, actually, the number of functions is quite limited. Only some 31 functions may be noted. The action of all tales included in our material develops within the limits of these functions. The same may also be said for the action of a great many other tales of the most dissimilar peoples. Further, if we read through all of the functions, one after another, we observe that one function develops out of another with logical and artistic necessity. We see that not a single function excludes another. They all belong to a single axis and not, as has already been mentioned, to a number of axes.

Now we shall give several individual, though highly important, deductions. We observe that a large number of functions are arranged in pairs (prohibition-violation, reconnaissance-delivery, struggle-victory, pursuit-deliverance, etc.). Other functions may be arranged according to groups. Thus villainy, dispatch, decision for counteraction, and departure from home

(ABC↑), constitute the complication. Elements DEF also form something of a whole. Alongside these combinations there are individual functions (absentations, punishment, marriage, etc.). We are merely noting these particular deductions at this point. The observation that functions are arranged in pairs will prove useful later, as well as the general deductions drawn here.

At this point we have to examine individual texts of the tales at close range. The question of how the given scheme applies to the texts, and what the individual tales constitute in relation to this scheme, can be resolved only by an analysis of the texts. But the reverse question, "What does the given scheme represent *in relation to the tales?*" can be answered here and now. The scheme is a *measuring unit* for individual tales. Just as cloth can be measured with a yardstick to determine its length, tales may be measured by the scheme and thereby defined. The application of the given scheme to various tales can also define the relationships of tales among themselves. We already foresee that the problem of kinship of tales, the problem of themes and variants, thanks to this, may receive a new solution.

NOTES

1. It is recommended that, prior to reading this chapter, one read through all the enumerated functions in succession without going into detail, taking note only of what is printed in capital letters. Such a cursory reading will make it easier to understand the thread of the account.
2. For what is meant by "magical agent" and "magical helper," cf. page 82.
3. The occasion will present itself further on for giving a more exact definition of the hero.
4. A more detailed account of the relationship between magical agents follows.
5. The problem of the connections of variants will be raised in the last chapter.
6. A curious rudiment of psychostasis.
7. The preliminary receipt of water could also be examined as a special form of F (receipt of a magical agent).

CHAPTER IV

Assimilations: Cases of the Double Morphological Meaning of a Single Function

It has already been shown that functions must be defined independently of the characters who are supposed to fulfill them. In following the enumeration of the functions, one becomes convinced that they must also be defined independently of how and in what manner they are fulfilled. This sometimes complicates the definition of individual cases, since different functions may be fulfilled in exactly the same way. Apparently we are confronted here with the influence of certain forms upon others. This phenomenon may be termed the assimilation of the means of fulfillment of functions.

This complicated phenomenon cannot be fully illuminated here. It can be examined only to the extent that this is necessary for subsequent analyses.

Let us examine a case in point (160): Iván asks a witch for a horse. She proposes that he select the best from a herd of identical colts. He chooses accurately and takes the horse. The action at the witch's house is a test of the hero by the donor, followed by the receipt of a magical agent. But in another tale (219), we see that the hero desires to wed the daughter of the water spirit who requires the hero to choose his bride from among twelve identical maidens. Can this case, as well, be defined as a *donor's* test? It is clear that in spite of the identical quality of the actions, we are confronted with a completely different element, namely, a difficult task connected with matchmaking. Assimilation of one form with another has taken place. Without concerning ourselves with the question of the priority of this or that particular meaning, we must nevertheless find the criterion which in all such cases would permit us to differentiate among elements without respect to similarity of actions. In these instances it is always possible to be governed by the principle of defining a function *according to its consequences.* If the receiving of a magical agent follows the solution of a task, then it is a case of the donor testing the hero (D^1). If the receipt of a bride and a marriage follow, then we have an example of the difficult task (M).

A difficult task can be distinguished from a dispatch of a complicational nature by the same method. The dispatch of someone in search of a deer with golden antlers, etc., also might be termed a "difficult task," but morphologically such a dispatch is a different element from a task set by a princess or a witch. If a dispatch gives rise to a departure, prolonged search (C↑), the meeting with a donor, etc., we have a complicational element (a, B, lack and dispatch). If a task is immediately solved and leads directly to marriage, we have M-N (a difficult task and its solution).

If marriage follows the fulfillment of a task, this means that the bride is earned or obtained through fulfillment of the task. In this manner the consequence of the task (and an element is defined according to its consequences) is the *acquisition of a sought-for person* or object (but not of a magical agent). Difficult tasks may be attested with matchmaking and apart from it. The latter case occurs very rarely (only twice in our material, tales 249, 239†). The obtaining of a person sought follows the solution of a task. Thus we come to the following summation: all tasks giving rise to a search must be considered in terms of B; all tasks giving rise to the receipt of a magical agent are considered as D. *All other tasks* are considered as M, with two varieties:

† "(v našem materiale liš' dva raza, No. 140, 132)" (p. 75). Although it is true that tale 140 (= new no. 249) contains difficult tasks not connected with matchmaking, tale 132 (= new no. 239) is not a clear illustration of the same thing. The latter contains at least a tacit assumption of matchmaking, since Iván marries the princess at the end of the tale, after she has failed to guess a third riddle posed by him. Also, a footnote at the beginning of the tale suggests that the princess will marry the man whose riddles she cannot guess. (There is the possibility here, of course, that the numerical reference is incorrect.) [L.A.W.]

tasks connected with match-making and marriage, and tasks not linked with matchmaking.

Let us look at a few more cases of simpler assimilations. Difficult tasks are the richest source for the most varied assimilations. A princess sometimes requires the building of a magical palace which the hero usually constructs immediately, with the help of a magical agent. Yet the building of a magical palace may also figure within the context of an entirely different meaning. After all his feats the hero builds a palace in the twinkling of an eye, and is revealed as a prince. This is a special type of transformation, apotheosis, and not the solution of a difficult task. One form has become assimilated with another, while the question of the primacy of the form, in either meaning, here again must remain open.

Finally, tasks may also be assimilated with dragon fighting. The fight with a dragon which has either kidnapped a girl or is ravaging a kingdom and the tasks given by a princess are completely different elements. But in a certain tale the princess demands that the hero conquer the dragon if he wants to obtain her hand in marriage. Should this case be considered as M (difficult task), or as H (struggle, fight)? This case amounts to a task since, first of all, a marriage follows, and secondly, struggle has been defined above as struggle *with a villain,* and the dragon in this instance is not the villain, but is introduced *ad hoc* and, without the slightest detriment to the course of the action, may be replaced by another kind of creature which must be either slain or tamed (compare the tasks of taming a horse, defeating a rival).

Other elements which also frequently assimilate are initial villainy and pursuit of the villain. Tale No. 93 begins with Iván's sister (a witch, also called a she-dragon) striving to devour her brother.† He flees from the house, and from this point the

† "Skazka No. 50 načinaetsja s togo, čto sestra Ivana (ved'ma, nazvana takže zmeixoj) stremitsja s"est' brata" (p. 76). This statement provokes two comments: first, in the tale itself (= new no. 93), the villain is everywhere referred to as the sister (*sestra*) or the witch (*ved'ma*) except in the last line, where she is called a *ved'ma-zmeja* (literally, "witch-serpent"). Apparently the author's contention that Iván's sister is really the sister of a dragon, transferred to the beginning of the tale, explains his referring to her in various places as a she-dragon (*zmeixa*): cf. pp. 52, 57, 86 in this translation.

Secondly, it should be noted that the tale does not begin with pursuit as such, but rather with a warning to Iván that his mother will soon give birth to a action develops. The sister of a dragon (a common pursuing character) is here transformed into the sister of the hero, and pursuit is transferred to the beginning of the tale and is used as A (villainy)—in particular, as A^{xvii}. If one compares in general how she-dragons act while giving chase with how a stepmother acts at the beginning of a tale, one will obtain parallels which shed a certain amount of light upon tale beginnings in which a stepmother torments her stepdaughter. Such a comparison becomes particularly sharp if one adds to it a study of the attributes of these characters. By introducing more material it can be shown that the stepmother is a she-dragon transferred to the beginning of the tale, who has taken on some traits of a witch and some ordinary characteristics. Persecution is sometimes directly comparable to pursuit. We will point out that the case of a she-dragon who transforms herself into an apple tree standing along the route travelled by the hero, attracting him with her exquisite but deadly fruit, may be readily compared with the stepmother's offer of poisoned apples which are sent to her stepdaughter. One can compare the transformation of a she-dragon into a beggar, and the transformation of a sorceress (sent by the stepmother) into a market woman, etc.

Another phenomenon resembling assimilation is the double morphological meaning of a single function. The simplest example of this is found in case No. 265. A prince sets off on a journey and forbids his wife to leave the house. There comes "a little old lady who seemed so sweet and simple. 'Why' says she, 'are you bored? If you would just have a look at God's world! If only you would walk through the garden!' " etc. (the persuasions of the villain, η^1). The princess goes out into the garden, thereby heeding the persuasions of the villain (θ^1), and simultaneously breaking an interdiction (δ^1). Thus the princess' exit from the house has a double morphological meaning. A second, more complicated example is found in tale No. 180,† and in others: Here, a difficult task (to kiss the princess while riding at

daughter who will be a terrible witch, etc. and that he had better flee. He does, and some time later (two-thirds of the way through the tale) he returns home and confronts his sister. It is from this point that the actual pursuit begins, as Iván flees again and his sister gives chase. [L.A.W.]

† The tale cited here (p. 77) is 105. More correctly, it should be 105b (= new no. 180). [L.A.W.]

full gallop) is transferred to the beginning of the tale. It gives rise to the hero's departure (i.e., falls into the class of the connective moment, B). It is characteristic that this task, given in the form of a call, is similar to the one uttered by the father of kidnapped princesses (cf.: "Who will kiss my daughter, Princess Milolíka, at full gallop . . ." etc.; "Who will seek out my daughters . . ." etc.) The call in both cases represents the same element (B^1); but in addition to this, the call in tale No. 180† is simultaneously a difficult task. Here, as in several similar cases, a difficult task is transferred to the complication and is used as element B, while at the same time still remaining M.

We consequently see that the means by which functions are fulfilled influence one another, and that identical forms adapt themselves to different functions. A certain form is transferred to a different position, acquiring a new meaning, or simultaneously retaining an old one. All of these phenomena complicate the analysis and require special attention when being compared to one another.

† The tale cited here (p. 77) is 105. More correctly, it should be 105b (= new no. 180). [L.A.W.]

CHAPTER V

Some Other Elements of the Tale

A. *Auxiliary Elements for the Interconnection of Functions*

Functions constitute the basic elements of the tale, those elements upon which the course of the action is built. Along with this there are component parts which, although they do not determine the development, are nevertheless very important.

We may observe that functions do not always follow one another in direct succession. If functions which follow one after another are performed by *different* characters, the second character must know all that has taken place up to that time. In connection with this, an entire system for the conveying of information has been developed in the tale, sometimes in very artistically striking forms. At times, this notification is absent from the tale, and then characters act either *ex machina* or are all-knowing. On the other hand, notification is sometimes employed where it is not at all necessary. These forms of notification serve to connect one function with another in the course of the action. For example, a princess kidnapped by Koščéj is seized and taken away. A chase ensues. The chase could immediately follow the seizure, but the tale inserts the words of Koščéj's horse: "Prince Iván came and he took with him Már'ja Mórevna," etc. Thus K is connected with Pr, attainment with pursuit (159). This is the simplest instance of notification. More artistically striking is the following form: a woman possessing magic apples has musical strings stretched on top of the wall. On his way back, Iván jumps over the wall and brushes against the strings, thereby informing the witch of the theft, and a chase ensues. Strings (as a connective between other functions) are used in the tale about the firebird, and in others.

Tales 106 and 108 present a more complicated case. Here the witch, instead of devouring Iván, has eaten up her own daughter. But she does not know it. From his hiding place, Iván laughingly informs her of this, after which flight and pursuit begin.†

We have the reverse instance when a person being chased must know that he is being pursued. He puts his ear to the ground and hears the pursuit.

A specific form for pursuit accompanied by the transformation of dragons' daughters or wives into gardens, wells, etc. is the following: Iván, having conquered a dragon and set out for home, returns once more. He overhears the she-dragons conversing and thus learns of the pursuit.

Such instances might be termed *direct notification*. Actually, B fits into this class, in particular B^4 (the announcement of misfortune), as well as ζ (the villain receives knowledge about the hero, or vice versa). But since these functions are important for the complication, they have assumed the nature of independent functions.

Notification is encountered in the intervals between the most varied functions. For example, an abducted princess sends a little dog to her parents with a letter indicating that Koženjáka can rescue her (villainy is linked with the dispatch of the hero—A and B). The tsar here learns about the hero. Similar information about the hero may be embellished with certain emotional tones. A specific form of this phenomenon is the slandering of the hero by those who envy him ("He brags that . . .," etc.), as a result of which the dispatching of the hero occurs. In other cases, the hero actually does boast of his strength (192). Complaints play the very same role in certain instances.

Sometimes such a notification assumes the character of a dialogue. The tale has developed canonical forms for a number of such dialogues. In order to hand over his magical gift, the donor must learn what has taken place beforehand. Thus we

† Flight and pursuit take place in tale 108, but not in 106. In the latter, the witch demands that Iván come down from his hiding place. He obliges, and then tricks the witch, pushing her into the stove. [L.A.W.]

have the witch's dialogue with Iván. The same is true in the case of a helper who, before acting in behalf of the hero, must know about the misfortune that has occurred; hence we have Iván's characteristic dialogue with his horse or with other helpers.

As varied as they are, the previous examples are nonetheless united by one general trait: in each case one character *finds out* something from another, and by this a preceding function is joined to the one following.

If, on the one hand, personages must first find out something (through direct announcement, an overheard conversation, sound signals, complaints, slanders, etc.) before beginning to act, then, on the other hand, they often fulfill their function because they see something. This creates a second species of connectives. Iván builds a palace opposite that of the tsar. The tsar sees him, and recognizes him as Iván. The marriage of his daughter to Iván follows. In this way T is connected with W. A spyglass is sometimes used in these and other cases. A similar role in connection with other functions is played by characters such as Čútkij ("Keen-ear") and Zórkij ("Sharp-eye").

If a needed object is very small or too far away, etc., a different means of connection is employed. The object (or person) is *brought:* an old man brings the tsar a bird (126); a herdsman brings the queen a crown (127); an archer brings the tsar a feather from the firebird (169); an old woman brings some linen to the tsar, and so forth. The most varied functions are connected in this way. In the tale about the firebird, Iván is brought before the tsar. The same thing applied in a different manner occurs in tale No. 145, in which a father brings his sons before the king. In the latter instance we have the connection not of two functions, but rather of an initial situation and a dispatch: the tsar is unmarried and seven clever men are brought to him. He dispatches them in search of a bride.

Closely connected with this, for example, is the *arrival* of the hero at the wedding of his betrothed, who had been claimed by the false hero. Thereby L (the pretensions of a deceiver) is connected with Q (recognition of the hero). But the same functions are joined even more vividly: all the beggars are invited to a celebration, and the hero appears among them, etc. The arrangement of great feasts also serves to link N (the solution of a task) with Q (recognition of the hero). The hero has solved a task assigned to him by the princess, but no one knows where he is. A feast is laid, and the princess makes the rounds of the guests; recognition follows. By this same method the princess exposes the false hero. A military inspection is decreed; the princess passes among the ranks and recognizes the imposter. The calling of a feast need not be considered a function. It is an auxiliary element in the linking of L or N with Q.

The enumerated five or six varieties have not been systematized here, nor do they exhaust the possibilities. But at present this is not necessary for our aims. We shall designate those elements serving to connect one function to another by the sign §.

B. *Auxiliary Elements in Trebling*

We have similar connective elements in various instances of trebling. Trebling, as such, has already been sufficiently elucidated in scholarly literature, and we need not dwell on this phenomenon here. We shall only mention that trebling may occur among individual details of an attributive nature (the three heads of a dragon), as well as among individual functions, pairs of functions (pursuit-rescue), groups of functions, and entire moves. Repetition may appear as a uniform distribution (three tasks, three years' service), as an accumulation (the third task is the most difficult, the third battle the worst), or may twice produce negative results before the third, successful outcome.

Sometimes action may simply be repeated mechanically; but at other times, to avoid a further development of the action, it is necessary to introduce certain elements which hold up the development and call for repetition. We will indicate a few examples: Iván receives a cudgel, or staff, or chain from his father. He tosses his cudgel into the air twice in a row (he snaps the chain). It shatters upon coming down. A new cudgel is ordered, but only a third proves suitable. The trying out of a magical agent cannot be considered as an independent function; it merely serves to motivate the receiving of the agent three times.

Iván encounters an old woman (a witch, a maiden), who sends him to her sister. The way from one sister to the other is shown by a ball of thread; the same thing occurs in tracing down a third sister. The guiding role of the ball of thread in this case is not function G^3. The ball merely leads from one donor to another, a situation which is motivated by the trebling of the form of the donor. It is altogether probable that this is its primary function, but along with this, the ball of thread also leads the hero to his point of destination; and then we have function G^3 before us.

We will indicate another example: in order that pursuit can be repeated, the villain must do away with the obstacle placed in his path by the hero. A witch gnaws through the forest, and a second chase begins. This act of gnawing cannot be counted among any of the 31 functions cited. It is an element which gives rise to a trebling, an element which links the first implementation with the second, or the second with the third. Side by side with this we have a form in which a witch simply gnaws on an oak tree in which Iván has taken refuge. Here an auxiliary element is employed in an independent meaning.

In like manner, if Iván while serving as a cook or groom conquers the first dragon and then returns to the kitchen, his return would not signify the function ↓; this return simply joins the first fight with the second and third. But if Iván returns home after the third fight having freed a princess, then we have the function ↓.

We shall designate with the sign ⁝ all elements serving to accomplish trebling.

C. *Motivations*

By motivations are meant both the reasons and the aims of personages which cause them to commit various acts. Motivations often add to a tale a completely distinctive, vivid coloring, but nevertheless motivations belong to the most inconstant and unstable elements of the tale. In addition, they represent an element less precise and definite than functions or connectives.

The majority of characters' acts in the middle of a tale are naturally motivated by the course of the action, and only villainy, as the first basic function of the tale, requires a certain supplementary motivation.

Here one may observe that completely identical or similar acts are motivated in the most varied ways. Expulsion and casting someone adrift are motivated by: a stepmother's hatred, a quarrel over an inheritance among brothers, envy, a fear of competition (Iván the merchant), an unequal marriage (Iván the peasant's son and a princess), suspicion of marital infidelity, a prophecy about a son's humiliation in the presence of his parents. In all of these cases expulsion is motivated by the greedy, evil, envious, suspicious character of the villain. But expulsion can be motivated by the unsavory character of the person exiled. Expulsion here assumes the nature of a certain form of justice. A son or grandson causes trouble or makes a fool of himself (tears off the arms and legs of passers-by). The townspeople complain (complaints—§), and the grandfather drives out his grandson.

Although the deeds of the exiled person constitute *action,* the tearing off of arms and legs cannot be considered as a function of the course of action. It is a *quality* of the hero, expressed in the acts which serve as the motive for his expulsion.

We notice that the actions of a dragon and of very many other villains are not in any way motivated by the tale. Of course, the dragon kidnaps the princess also because of certain motives (for the purpose of a forced marriage or in order to devour her), but the tale says nothing about this. There is reason to think that motivations formulated in words are alien to the tale on the whole, and that motivations in general may be considered with a great degree of probability as new formations.

In those tales in which no villainy is present, the function *a* (lack) serves as its counterpart, while B (dispatch) appears as the first function. One may observe that a dispatch because of lack is also motivated in the most varied ways.

An initial shortage or lack represents a situation. One can imagine that, prior to the beginning of the action, the situation has lasted for years. But the moment comes when the dispatcher or searcher suddenly realizes that something is lacking, and this moment is dependent upon a motivation causing dispatch (B), or an immediate search (C↑).

The realization of a lack may happen in the following way: the object lacking involuntarily gives away some bit of news about itself by appearing momentarily, leaving behind some clear trace of itself, or else appearing to the hero in certain reflected forms (portraits, stories). The hero (or the dispatcher) loses his mental equilibrium and is seized with a longing for the beauty which he had once beheld; from this the whole action develops. The firebird and the feather which it leaves behind constitute one of the most characteristic and excellent examples: "This feather was so marvelous and so bright that if you brought it into a dark room it would shine as though a great many candles had been lit there."[1] A similar example begins tale No. 138. Here the tsar dreams of a wonderful horse. "Each hair of this horse was silver, and on his forehead there shone a moon." The tsar sends for the horse. In relation to a princess, this element may be colored differently. A soldier sees Eléna passing by: "and the sky and the ground were lit up. A golden chariot flew through the air, and harnessed to it were six fiery dragons. Eléna the Wise sat in the chariot. Her beauty is so indescribable that one cannot imagine it, nor can it be guessed, nor told in a tale. She alighted from the chariot, sat down upon a golden throne, and began to beckon the doves to her, each in his turn, and to teach them all manner of wise things [waiting doves have been mentioned earlier]. When she ended her teaching, she hopped up into her chariot and disappeared." (236). The soldier falls in love with Eléna, etc. Here one can also include those instances in which a hero sees the portrait of an exceptionally beautiful girl in a forbidden closet and falls fatally in love with her.

We see further that a lack is realized through intermediary personages who call Iván's attention to the fact that he lacks something or other. Most often these are parents who discover that their son needs a bride. This same role is played by stories concerning exceptionally beautiful women, such as the following: "Ah, Prince Iván, what kind of beauty am I? For beyond thrice nine lands, in the thrice ninth kingdom there lives with a dragon tsar a queen, and she is a beauty truly beyond description" (161). These and similar stories (about princesses, knights, miracles, etc.) give rise to a quest.

A lack may at times be imaginary. An evil sister or mother, a wicked master, or a wicked king send Iván after this or that wonder, which they do not need, but which merely serves as a pretext for getting rid of him. A merchant sends him off because he fears his strength, a tsar because he wants to possess his wife, and evil sisters because of a dragon's flattery. Similar dispatches are sometimes motivated by imaginary illness. In these instances there is no direct villainy, and departure logically (though not morphologically) takes its place, assuming the character of villainy. A dragon stands behind the back of an evil sister, and the dispatcher is generally subjected to the same punishments undergone by a villain in other tales. We may remark that dispatch of a hostile nature and dispatch of a friendly character develop in quite the same manner. Whether Iván sets out to obtain a wonderful object because his evil sister or a wicked tsar wants to deceive him, or because his father is ill, or because the father has dreamed of a wonderful thing—all this has no influence on the structure of the course of action, i.e., on the search as such, as we shall see later. One may observe in general that the feelings and intentions of the dramatis personae do not have an effect on the course of action in any instances at all.

There are a great many ways by which a lack is realized. Envy, poverty (for rationalized forms), the daring and strength of the hero, and many other things can call forth a quest. Even a desire to have children may create an independent move (the hero is dispatched in order to search for the remedy for childlessness). This occurrence is very interesting. It shows that any tale element (in this case, the tsar's lack of children) can, as it were, accumulate action, can evolve into an independent story, or can cause one. But like any living thing, the tale can generate only forms that resemble itself. If any cell of a tale organism becomes a small tale within a larger one, it is built, as we shall see later, according to the same rules as any fairy tale.

A feeling of shortage is also often not motivated by anything at all. The tsar calls his children together, saying, "Do me a service," etc., and sends them out on a quest.

NOTE

1. Unfortunately, in our material there are no completely analogous cases for the realization of the lack of a princess. We are reminded of Isolde's golden hair which is brought to King Mark by swallows. An unusually fragrant strand of hair washed up on the seashore has the same meaning in African tales. In an ancient Greek tale an eagle brings a king the slipper of a beautiful hetaera.

CHAPTER VI

The Distribution of Functions Among Dramatis Personae

Although functions, as such, are the subjects of the present study (and not their performers nor the objects dependent upon them), we nevertheless should examine the question of how functions are distributed among the dramatis personae. Before answering this question in detail, one might note that many functions logically join together into certain *spheres*. These spheres in toto correspond to their respective performers. They are spheres of action. The following spheres of action are present in the tale:

1. The sphere of action of the *villain*. Constituents: villainy (A); a fight or other forms of struggle with the hero (H); pursuit (Pr).
2. The sphere of action of the *donor* (provider). Constituents: the preparation for the transmission of a magical agent (D); provision of the hero with a magical agent (F).
3. The sphere of action of the *helper*. Constituents: the spatial transference of the hero (G); liquidation of misfortune or lack (K); rescue from pursuit (Rs); the solution of difficult tasks (N); transfiguration of the hero (T).
4. The sphere of action of a *princess* (a sought-for person) and of *her father*. Constituents: the assignment of difficult tasks (M); branding (J); exposure (Ex); recognition (Q); punishment of a second villain (U); marriage (W). The princess and her father cannot be exactly delineated from each other ac-

cording to functions. Most often it is the father who assigns difficult tasks due to hostile feeling toward the suitor. He also frequently punishes (or orders punished) the false hero.

5. The sphere of action of the *dispatcher*. Constituent: dispatch (connective incident, B).
6. The sphere of action of the *hero*. Constituents: departure on a search (C↑); reaction to the demands of the donor (E); wedding (W*). The first function (C) is characteristic of the seeker-hero; the victim-hero performs only the remaining functions.
7. The sphere of action of the *false hero* also includes C↑, followed by E and, as a specific function, L.

Consequently, the tale evidences seven dramatis personae. The functions of the preparatory section (β,γ-δ,ε-ζ,η-θ) are also distributed among the same characters, but the distribution here is unequal, making the definition of the characters impossible by these functions. In addition, there exist special personages for connections (complainers, informers, slanderers), and also special betrayers for function ζ (a looking glass, a chisel, a broom). Personages such as "One-Eye," "Two-Eye," and "Three-Eye" belong here also.

The problem of the distribution of functions may be resolved on the plane of the problem concerning the distribution of the *spheres of action* among the characters.

How are the above-mentioned spheres of action distributed among individual tale characters? There are three possibilities here:

1. The sphere of action exactly corresponds to the character. The witch who tests and rewards the hero, and animals begging for mercy and giving Iván a gift, are pure donors. The horse which brings Iván to the princess, helps in abducting her, solves a difficult task, rescues the hero from pursuit, etc., is a pure helper.

2. One character is involved in several spheres of action. The little iron peasant who asks to be let out of a tower, thereupon rewarding Iván with strength and a magic tablecloth, but who eventually also aids in killing the dragon, is simultaneously both a donor and a helper. The category of grateful animals demands special scrutiny. They begin as donors (begging for help or mercy), then they place themselves at the disposal of the hero

and become his helpers. This case has already been noted in Chapter III (F^9). Sometimes it happens that an animal which has been freed or spared by the hero simply disappears without even informing the hero of the formula to summon it, but in a critical moment it appears in the role of a helper. It rewards the hero with *direct action*. It may, for example, help the hero get to another kingdom, or it obtains for him the object of his search, and so on. Cases of this type may be designated as $F^9 = G$, $F^9 = K$, etc.

Special attention should also be devoted to the witch (or any other inhabitant of a forest hut) who fights with Iván and then runs off, thereby showing Iván the way to the other world. Guidance is a function of the helper, and therefore the witch plays the role of an involuntary (and even unwilling) helper. She begins as an antagonistic donor and then becomes an involuntary helper.

Several other cases of combination can be cited. The father who dispatches his son, giving him a cudgel, is at the same time both a dispatcher and a donor. The three maidens in golden, silver, and bronze palaces who present Iván with a magical ring, etc., and then marry the heroes, are donors and princesses. The witch who kidnaps a boy, places him in her oven, and is then robbed by the boy (a magic kerchief is stolen from her) combines the functions of villain and (unintentional, hostile) donor. Thus once again we come upon the phenomenon that the will of personages, their intentions, cannot be considered as an essential motif for their definition. The important thing is not what they want to do, nor how they feel, but their deeds as such, evaluated and defined from the viewpoint of their meaning for the hero and for the course of the action. Here we obtain the same picture as that in analyzing motivations: the feelings of a dispatcher (be they hostile, neutral or friendly) do not influence the course of the action.

3. The reverse case: a single sphere of action is distributed among several characters. For example, if a dragon is killed in a battle, it is incapable of pursuit. For the pursuit, special personages are introduced: wives, daughters, sisters, mothers-in-law, and mothers of dragons—his female relations. Elements D, E, and F are sometimes similarly distributed, although such a distribution more often than not proves artistically unsuccess-

ful. One character does the testing while another one accidentally gives the reward. We have already seen that the functions of a princess are distributed between herself and her father. However, this phenomenon generally involves helpers. Here we should first of all dwell upon the relationship between magical agents and magical helpers. Let us compare the following examples: (1) Iván receives a flying carpet on which he flies either to a princess or home; (2) Iván obtains a horse on which he flies either to a princess or home. Hence it is apparent that *objects act in the same way as do living things.* Thus a cudgel by itself kills all of the enemies and punishes thieves, etc. Further comparisons: (1) Iván receives an eagle as a present, and on it he flies away; (2) Iván receives the gift of being able to transform himself into a falcon, and in the form of a falcon he flies away. Another comparison: Iván receives a horse which can scatter (defecate) gold, and it makes Iván a rich man. On the other hand: Iván eats a bird's giblets and receives the ability to spit up gold, becoming a rich man. It is evident from these two examples that *a quality functions as a living thing.* In this manner living things, objects, and qualities, from the morphological point of view, founded upon the functions of the dramatis personae, must be examined as equivalent quantities. However, it is more convenient to term living things "magical helpers" and objects and qualities as "magical agents," even though they both function in exactly the same manner.

This identity is, however, subject to certain limitations. Three categories of helpers may be ascertained: (1) universal helpers capable of fulfilling (in certain ways) all five functions of the helper: in our material only the steed conforms to these qualifications; (2) partial helpers capable of fulfilling several functions (although not all of the five given): here belong various animals (other than the horse), spirits appearing out of rings, various tempters, etc.; (3) specific helpers, fulfilling only a single function. Only objects belong in this last category: the ball of thread serves as a guide; the magic sword serves to defeat the enemy; the self-playing gusla aids in accomplishing the princess' task, and so forth. Hence it is apparent that the magical agent is actually nothing more than a particular form of magical helper.

One should also make mention of the fact that the hero often gets along without any helpers. He is his own helper, as it were.

But if we had the opportunity to study attributes, it would be possible to show that in these instances the hero takes on not only the functions of the helper, but his attributes as well. One of the most important attributes of a helper is his prophetic wisdom: the prophetic horse, the prophetic wife, the wise lad, etc. When a helper is absent from a tale, this quality is transferred to the hero. The result is the appearance of the prophetic hero.

Conversely, a helper at times may perform those functions which are specific for the hero. Besides C, the only thing which is specific for him is his reaction to the activity of the donor. Yet here the helper often acts instead of the hero: mice play a game of blind man's buff with a bear and win; grateful animals in place of Iván perform the tasks assigned by a witch (98, 160).†

† The original textual references (p. 92) are to tales 94 and 95. Number 94 is incorrect. However, in tale 54 (= new no. 98) we find a situation in which a mouse takes a maiden's place in a game of blind man's buff with a bear and wins. [L.A.W.]

CHAPTER VII

Ways in Which New Characters Are Introduced into the Course of Action

Each category of characters has its own form of appearing. Each category employs certain means to introduce a character into the course of action. These forms are the following:

The *villain* appears twice during the course of action. First he makes a sudden appearance from outside (flies to the scene, sneaks up on someone, etc.), and then disappears. His second appearance in the tale is as a person *who has been sought out,* usually as the result of guidance.

The *donor* is encountered accidentally, most often in the forest (in a hut), or else in a field, on the roadway, in the street.

The *magical helper* is introduced as a gift. This moment is designated as F, and its possible variations have been described earlier.

The *dispatcher,* the *hero,* the *false hero,* as well as the *princess* are introduced into the initial situation. The false hero is sometimes not mentioned among the enumerated dramatis personae in the initial situation, and only later is it made known that he lives at court or in the house. The princess, like the villain, appears twice within the tale. The second time, she is introduced as a personage who has been sought out. Here the seeker may either see her first and then see the villain (a dialogue with the princess while the dragon is not home), or vice versa.

This distribution may be considered as the norm of the tale. But deviations do occur. If a donor is missing from a tale, the forms of his appearance are transferred to the next character in line; namely, to the helper. Thus various tempters are accidentally encountered by the hero in the manner in which he would meet a donor. If a character operates in two spheres of functions, he is introduced in those forms in which he first begins to act. The wise wife who appears at first as a donor, and later as a helper and as a princess, is introduced as a donor rather than as a helper or princess.

Another deviation exists in the fact that all characters may be introduced via the initial situation. As has already been shown, this form is specific only for heroes, for a dispatcher, and for a princess. One may distinguish two basic forms of initial situations: (1) a situation including the *seeker* together with his family (a father and his three sons); (2) a situation including the villain's *victim,* together with his family (the tsar's three daughters). Some tales give both situations. If a tale begins with a lack, a situation with a seeker (and sometimes also a dispatcher) is needed. These situations may even merge with each other. But since an initial situation always demands the presence of the members of a single family, the seeker and the person sought are transformed from Iván and the princess into a brother and sister, into sons and their mother, etc. Such a situation includes both the seeker and the villain's victim.[1]

Certain situations of this type are handled in an epic manner. In the beginning the seeker is not at hand. He is born, usually in some miraculous manner. The miraculous birth of the hero is a very important narrative element. It is one of the forms of the hero's appearance and this form is included in the initial situation. The hero's birth is usually accompanied by a prophecy concerning his destiny. Even before the complication begins he shows the attributes of a future hero. His rapid growth and his superiority over his brothers are described. Sometimes, conversely, Iván is a numskull. All of the hero's attributes cannot be studied by us. Certain of them are expressed in deeds (a quarrel over primacy). These acts do not, however, constitute functions of the course of action.

Let us again recall that the initial situation often presents a picture of unusual, sometimes emphasized, prosperity, often in quite vivid, beautiful forms. This prosperity serves as a contrasting background for the ensuing misfortune. Into this situation the tale sometimes introduces a donor, a helper, and a villain. Special attention need be paid only to those situations which include a villain. Since the situation always requires the introduction of members of one family, the villain included in the initial situation is transformed into a relative of the hero, in spite of the fact that his attributes might plainly coincide with those of a dragon, a witch, etc. The witch in tale No. 93, for example, is a typical she-dragon. But upon her transference to the initial situation, she becomes the hero's sister.†

The situations in second, and repeated moves in general, should be mentioned. These second moves similarly begin with a given situation. If Iván has obtained a bride and a magical agent, and the princess (who is often already his wife) then steals this magical agent, we have the following situation: villain +seeker+future object of a search. Thus in second moves the villain is encountered in the initial situation more often. One and the same person can play one role in the first move and quite another role in the second (a devil as helper in the first move, but as villain in the second, etc.). All the characters of the first move who later take part in the second are already present, are already known to the audience or to the reader; therefore, there is no need for a new appearance of personages belonging to the corresponding category. However, it does happen, for example, that during a second move a storyteller will forget about the helper of the first move and will make the hero find one all over again.

The situation introducing a stepmother also requires special mention. The stepmother is either present from the very beginning, or the story of an old man's remarriage after the death of his first wife is recounted. Through the old man's second marriage the villain is introduced into the tale. Evil daughters or false heroes are then born.

All of the preceding questions may be elaborated upon in greater detail, but the indications given here are sufficient for purposes of a general morphology.

† Cf. the footnote on p. 68. [L.A.W.]

NOTE

1. One may observe that in such tales the princess is the last person to be introduced. Ivan sets out in search of his mother, who has been abducted by Koščéj, and he finds the tsar's daughter, who has also been kidnapped by Koščéj.

CHAPTER VIII

On the Attributes of Dramatis Personae and their Significance

The study of characters according to their functions, their distribution into categories, and their forms of appearance inevitably leads us to the problem of tale characters in general. Previously, we sharply separated the question of *who* acts in the tale from the question of the actions themselves. The nomenclature and attributes of characters are variable quantities of the tale. By attributes we mean the totality of all the external qualities of the characters: their age, sex, status, external appearance, peculiarities of this appearance, and so forth. These attributes provide the tale with its brilliance, charm, and beauty. When one speaks of a tale, he first recalls, of course, Bába Jagá and her hut, many-headed dragons, Prince Iván and the beautiful princess, magical flying horses, and many other things. We have seen, however, that one character in a tale is easily replaced by another. These substitutions have their own, sometimes very complicated, causes. Real life itself creates new, vivid images which supplant tale personages. The epos of neighboring peoples exerts its influence, as does written literature, religion (Christianity for example), and local beliefs. The tale at its core preserves traces of very ancient paganism, of ancient customs and rituals. The tale gradually undergoes a metamorphosis, and these transformations and metamorphoses of tales are also subject to certain laws. It is all these processes that create a multiformity which is exceptionally difficult to analyze.

Nevertheless, analysis is possible. The constancy of functions endures, permitting us to also introduce into our system those elements which become grouped around the functions.

How does one create this system? The best method is to make up tables. Veselóvskij long ago spoke of a tabulation of tales—although he did not greatly believe in its possibility.

Such tables have been formulated by us. There is no opportunity to acquaint the reader with all of the details of these tables, even though they are not especially complicated. The study of a character's attributes establishes only the following three basic headings: external appearance and nomenclature, particularities of introduction into the narrative, and dwelling place. To these are added a series of other, less significant, auxiliary elements. Thus, characteristic peculiarities of Bába Jagá are: her name, her appearance (her bony leg, her "nose which has grown to the ceiling," etc.), her hut turning on chicken legs, and the manner of her entrance: she flies down in a mortar accompanied by whistling and noise. If a character is defined from the viewpoint of his functions, for example, as a donor, helper, etc., and the heading in the table includes everything mentioned about him, then an exceedingly interesting picture is obtained. All of the material under one heading may be examined entirely independently for all the tale material. Although these quantities represent variable elements, here too one observes a great deal of repetition. The most often repeated and most striking forms represent a particular canonical tale pattern. This pattern can be delineated, but in order to do so, one first has to determine how to distinguish the basic forms from those which are either derivative or heteronymous. There exist international canonical patterns as well as national forms (peculiarly Indic, Arabic, Russian, German, etc.) and provincial forms (those from the Far North, Novgorod, Perm, Siberia, and so forth). Finally, forms exist which are grouped according to certain social categories: soldier, farm labor, and semi-urban. Further, we may observe that an element which is usually encountered under one heading might suddenly be met under a totally different one; here we have a transposition of forms. A dragon, for example, may play the role of donor-counselor. Transpositions of this kind play a great role in the creation of tale formations. These formations often are taken for a new theme, although they are derived from old ones as the result of a certain transformation or metamorphosis. Transposition is not the only type of transformation. By grouping the material of each heading, we can define all methods, or more precisely, all types of transformations. We shall not take up these types of transformations, since this would lead us too far astray. Transformations constitute material for an independent investigation.

But the composing of tables and the study of the attributes of dramatis personae, as well as the study of variables, generally allows something else as well. We already know that a tale is constructed on the basis of identical functions. Attributive elements are not alone in being subject to the laws of transformation. Functions are equally subject to them, although this is less apparent since they are less conducive to analytical study. (Those forms which we consider basic are, in our enumeration, always listed as the first forms.) If we were to devote a special investigation to this question, it would be possible to construct the archetype of the fairy tale not only schematically, as we do here, but concretely as well. This has actually been done for quite some time in the case of individual themes. Rejecting all local, secondary formations, and leaving only the fundamental forms, we shall obtain that one tale with respect to which all fairy tales will appear as variants. The investigations we have carried out in this regard have led us to those tales in which a dragon kidnaps a princess, in which Iván meets a witch, obtains a steed, flies away, vanquishes the dragon with the help of the steed, returns, is subjected to pursuit by she-dragons, meets his brothers, etc. These investigations have also led us to the basic form of fairy tales in general. However, it is possible to prove this only with the help of a precise study of the metamorphoses, that is, of the transformations of tales. With regard to formal questions, this will eventually lead us to the question of themes and variants and of the relationship of themes to composition.

Yet the study of attributes leads us to another highly important consequence. If one extracts all the basic forms for each heading and unites them into one tale, such a tale will reveal that certain abstract representations lie at its core.

Let us explain this idea more precisely with an example. If all the tasks of the donor are registered under one heading, we see that these tasks are not accidental. From the point of view of the narration as such, they are nothing more than one of the devices of epic retardation: an obstacle is placed before the hero, in the surmounting of which he receives the means for the attainment of his goal. From this point of view it does not matter what the task itself may be. Indeed, many such tasks should be considered only as components of a certain artistic composition. But in relation to the basic forms of tasks it is possible to observe that they possess a particular, hidden goal. The question, "What exactly does the witch (or another donor) want to find out from the hero, and what does she test in him?" allows a *single* solution which will be expressed in an abstract formula. A formula of this same type, though different in substance, sheds light upon the tasks of the princess. In comparing formulae, we observe that the one develops out of the other. In contrasting these formulae with other attributive elements, we unexpectedly get the same connected chain in the logical plan of the tale as in the artistic plan. Iván's lying on the stove (an international and not at all Russian feature), his connection with his dead parents, the content of prohibitions and their violation, the task given by the donor to guard something (basic form: to guard the witch's hut), even such details as the golden hair of the princess (a feature distributed over the entire world) acquire a very special meaning and lend themselves to analysis. The study of attributes makes possible a scientific *interpretation* of the tale. From the historical point of view, this signifies that the fairy tale in its morphological bases represents a *myth*. We fully realize that, from the point of view of contemporary scholarship, we are expressing a totally heretical idea. This idea has been considerably discredited by adherents of the mythological school. On the other hand, this idea has such strong supporters as Wundt, and now we are coming to it by way of morphological analysis.

However, we are stating all of this in the form of a supposition. Morphological investigations in this sphere should be linked with a historical study, which at present cannot enter into our task. Here the tale must be studied in regard to religious notions.

Thus we see that the study of the attributes of dramatis personae, barely outlined here, is of great importance. An exact distribution of dramatis personae according to their attributes is not part of our task. To speak of the fact that the villain may be a dragon, a witch, an old hag, robbers, merchants, or an evil princess, etc., or that the donor may be a witch, an old woman, a backyard-grandma (*bábuška-zadvorěnka*), a forest-spirit, or a bear, etc., is not worthwhile, because this would lead to the compiling of a catalogue. Such a catalogue is interesting only if it is presented from the standpoint of more general problems. These problems have been outlined; they are: the laws of transformations and the abstract concepts which are reflected in the basic forms of these attributes. We have also given a system, a plan of elaboration.[1] But since the general questions thus formulated demand special investigations and cannot be resolved in our brief essay, a simple catalogue loses its over-all meaning and becomes a dry list—quite necessary for the specialist but not of wide interest.

NOTE

1. Cf. Appendix I.

CHAPTER IX

The Tale as a Whole

A. *The Ways in Which Stories are Combined*

Now that the main elements of the tale have been indicated and several attendant features have been clarified, we may proceed to break down the texts into their components.

First of all, at this point the question arises as to what is meant by a tale.

Morphologically, a tale (*skázka*) may be termed any development proceeding from villainy (A) or a lack (*a*), through intermediary functions to marriage (W*), or to other functions employed as a dénouement. Terminal functions are at times a reward (F), a gain or in general the liquidation of misfortune (K), an escape from pursuit (Rs), etc. This type of development is termed by us a *move* (*xod*). Each new act of villainy, each new lack creates a new move. One tale may have several moves, and when analyzing a text, one must first of all determine the number of moves of which it consists. One move may directly follow another, but they may also interweave; a development which has begun pauses, and a new move is inserted. Singling out a move is not always an easy matter, but it is always possible with complete exactitude. However, if we have conditionally defined the tale as a move, this still does not mean that the number of moves corresponds exactly to the number of tales. Special devices of parallelism, repetitions, etc., lead to the fact that one tale may be composed of several moves.

Therefore, before solving the problem of how to distinguish

a text containing one tale from a text containing two or more, let us see by what methods the moves are combined, regardless of the number of tales in a text.

The combination of moves may be as follows:

1. One move directly follows another. An approximate scheme of such combinations is:

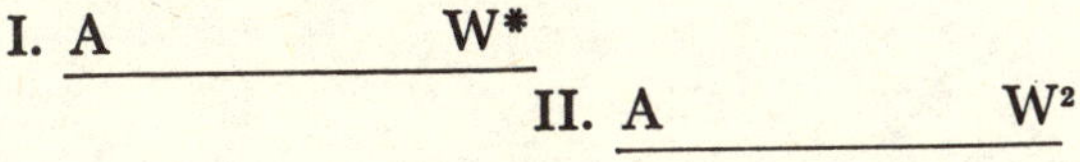

2. A new move begins before the termination of the first one. Action is interrupted by an episodic move. After the completion of the episode, the completion of the first move follows as well. The scheme is:

3. An episode may also be interrupted in its turn, and in this case fairly complicated schemes may result.

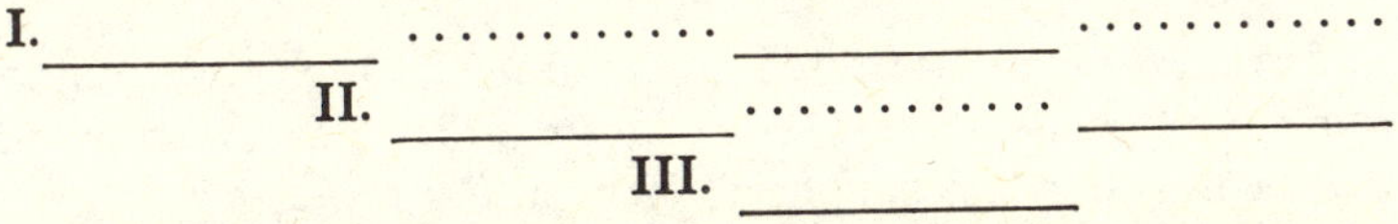

4. A tale may begin with two villainies at once, of which the first one may be liquidated completely before the other is. If the hero is killed and a magical agent is stolen from him, then first of all the murder is liquidated, and then the theft is liquidated also.

5. Two moves may have a common ending.

6. Sometimes a tale contains *two* seekers (see No. 155, "The Two Iváns, Soldier's Sons"). The heroes part in the middle of the first move. They usually part with omens at a road marker. This road marker serves as a *disuniting* element. (Parting at a road marker we shall designate by the sign <.

Sometimes, however, the road marker amounts to a simple accessory.) On parting, the heroes often give one another an object: a signaller (a spoon, a looking glass, a kerchief). We shall designate the transference of a signalling object with the sign Y. The schemes of such tales are:

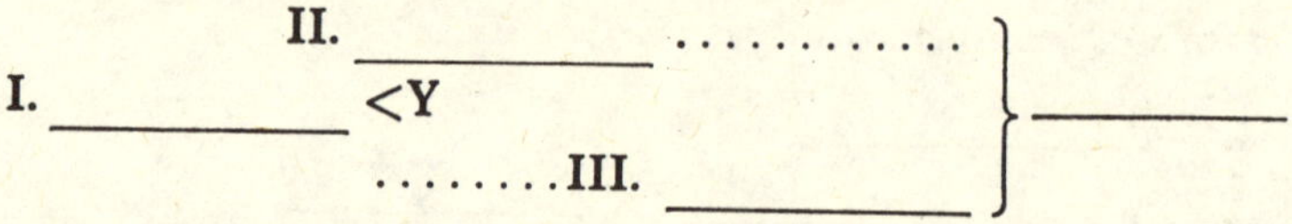

These are the chief methods of combining moves. The question is raised: under what conditions do several moves form a single tale, and when are we confronted by two or more tales? At this point it must first of all be said that *the method of combining moves does not exert any influence whatever*. No clear-cut indications exist. But several of the more lucid cases may be cited.

A *single* tale is present in the following instances:

1. If the entire tale consists of one move.

2. If the tale consists of two moves, one of which ends positively and the other negatively. For example, first move: a stepmother drives out her stepdaughter; her father takes her away; she returns with gifts. Second move: the stepmother dispatches her daughters; the father takes them away, and they return punished.

3. In the event of the trebling of entire moves. A dragon abducts a girl. First and second moves: elder brothers set out, in turn, to look for her and become stuck. Third move: the youngest brother sets out and rescues the girl and his brothers.

4. If a magical agent is obtained in the first move and is used only in the second. For example, first move: brothers set out from home to obtain horses for themselves. They get them and return. Second move: a dragon threatens a princess. The brothers set forth. They reach their goal with the help of the horses. Here, apparently, the following has occurred: the obtaining of the magical agent, which is usually placed in the middle of the tale, is placed before the main complication (the menace of the dragon). The obtaining of the magical agent is preceded

by an unmotivated realization of a lack—the brothers suddenly want horses, thereby provoking a quest, i.e., a move.

5. We also have a single tale if, up to the conclusive liquidation of misfortune, there is suddenly sensed some sort of shortage or lack which provokes a new quest, i.e. a new move, but not a new tale. In such cases a new horse, the egg containing Koščéj's death, etc., are needed, which also provides the beginning for a new development, while the development which has already commenced temporarily pauses.

6. We also have a single tale in the case where two villainous acts are present together in the complication (the banishment and bewitching of a stepdaughter, and so on).

7. A single tale is also evident in texts where the first move includes a fight with a dragon, and the second move begins with the theft of the booty by brothers, the casting of the hero into a chasm, etc.; L then follows, as do difficult tasks. This is the development which became clear to us during the enumeration of all functions of the tale. This is the most complete and perfect form of the tale.

8. Tales in which the heroes part at a road marker may also be considered as integral (*cél'nye*) tales. It must be noted, however, that each brother's fate may form a completely separate tale, and it is possible that this case should be excluded from the category of integral tales.

In all other cases we have two or more tales. When defining double tales, one must not allow oneself to become misled by very brief moves. Especially brief are the moves which include crop damage and a declaration of war. In general, crop damage occupies a somewhat special place. For the most part, it is immediately evident that the character who damages the crop plays a bigger role in the second move than in the first, and that through crop damage he is merely introduced. Thus in tale No. 105 the mare that steals the hay is subsequently the donor (compare No. 186 and No. 187 as well). In tale No. 126 the brass peasant is introduced in the form of a little bird who is stealing grain; he is analogous to the peasant of tales No. 123 and No. 125. ("And that birdie—that was the brass peasant.") But a division of tales which is set up on the basis of the appearance of characters is impossible. Otherwise, it might be possible to say that each first move only prepares and introduces characters for the following move. The stealing of crops and the capture of the thief is, theoretically, a completely separate tale. But for the most part such a move is felt to be introductory.

B. *An Example of Analysis of a Tale*

Knowing how moves are distributed, we can decompose any tale into its components. We recall that the functions of the dramatis personae are the basic components. Subsequently, we have the conjunctive elements, and then motivations. The forms of appearance of the dramatis personae (the flying arrival of a dragon, the meeting with a witch) occupy a special place. Finally, we have the attributive elements or accessories, such as a witch's hut or her clay leg. These five categories of elements define not only the construction of a tale, but the tale as a whole.

Let us try to decompose a tale completely, word for word. As an example we shall select a brief, single-move tale—the shortest one of our material. Illustrative analyses of more complicated tales are provided in Appendix II, since they are important, on the whole, only for the specialist.

The tale is that of "The Swan-Geese" (No. 113).[1]

There lived an old man and an old woman; they had a daughter and a little son.[1]	1. Initial situation (α).
"Daughter, daughter," said the mother, "we are going out to work and we will bring you back a little bun, sew you a little dress and buy you a little kerchief. Be wise, take care of your little brother, and do not leave the courtyard."[2]	2. Interdiction, intensified with promises (γ).
The elders went away,[3]	3. Departure of the elders (β^1).
and the daughter forgot what they had ordered[4] her to do. She placed her little brother on the grass under a window and ran out	4. Violation of the interdiction is motivated (M).

into the street and became absorbed in playing and having fun.[5]

The swan-geese flew down, seized the little boy and carried him away on their wings.[6]

The little girl came back, looked, but her brother wasn't there.[7] She gasped and rushed hither and thither, but he wasn't anywhere. She called out; she burst into tears, wailing that harm would come to her from her father and her mother, but her little brother did not answer.[8] She ran out into the open field;[9] the swan-geese sped away into the distance and disappeared beyond the dark wood. The swan-geese had long before acquired an ill fame, caused much mischief, and had stolen many a little child. The girl guessed that they had carried off her little brother, and she set out to catch up with them.[10] She ran and ran until she came upon a stove.[11]

"Stove, stove, tell me: where have the geese flown?"

"If you eat my little ryecake, I'll tell."[12] "Oh, we don't even eat cakes made of wheat in my father's house."[13] (A meeting with an apple tree and a river follows. Similar proposals and similar insolent replies.)

She would have run through

5. Violation of the interdiction (δ^1).
6. Villainy (A^1).
7. Rudiment of the announcement of misfortune (B^4).
8. Detailing: rudiment of trebling.
9. Departure from home on a quest ($C\uparrow$).
10. Since no dispatcher is present to inform of the misfortune, this role is transferred to the villain himself, after a certain delay, who provides information about the nature of the misfortune by the fact that he shows himself for a second.
11. Appearance of the tester, met accidentally (a canonical form of his appearance) (71, 73).
12. Dialogue with the tester (very abbreviated) and the trial (76, 78b).
13. An insolent answer, negative reaction of the hero. This result provokes a trebled repetition. It is necessary for the course of action that the hero be given help (E neg.).

the fields and wandered in the forest a long time if she had not by good fortune met a hedgehog.[14] She wished to nudge him,[15] but was afraid of pricking herself.[16] "Little hedgehog, little hedgehog," she asked, "did you not see where the geese have flown?"[17] "Away, over there," he pointed.[18]

She ran and came upon a hut on chicken legs. It was standing and turning around.[19]

In the hut sat Bába Jagá, hag-faced and with a leg of clay.[20] The little brother also sat there on a little bench,[21] playing with golden apples.[22]

His sister saw him, stole up, seized him and carried him away,[23,24] and the geese flew after her in pursuit;[25] the evil-doers were overtaking them; where was there to hide?

(Once again a triple testing by the same characters, but with a positive answer which evokes the aid of the tester himself in the form of rescue from pursuit. The river, the apple tree, and the stove hide the little girl.[26] The tale ends with the little girl's arrival home.)

14. Appearance of the thankful helper (F_6^9).
15. Helpless status of the helper without a request for mercy (d^7).
16. Mercy (E^7).
17. Dialogue (§).
18. The thankful hedgehog becomes a helper who shows the way ($F^9 = G^4$).
19. Dwelling of the villain (92b).
20. Physical appearance of the villain (94).
21. Appearance of the sought-for personage (98).
22. Gold is one of the typical details of a sought-for personage. Attribute (99).
23. Receipt, through the application of cunning or strength (K^1).
24. Return is implied but not mentioned (↓).
25. Pursuit, chase in the form of flight (Pr^1).
26. Deliverance from pursuit (Rs^4).

If one were now to write out all functions of this tale, the following scheme would result:

$$\gamma^1\beta^1\delta^1A^1C\uparrow\left\{\begin{matrix}[DE^1\text{ neg. }F\text{ neg.}]\\ \\ d^7E^7F^9\end{matrix}\right\}G^4K^1\downarrow[Pr^1D^1E^1F^9=Rs^4]^3$$

Now let us imagine that all the tales in our material are analyzed in a similar manner and that a scheme is made as a result of each analysis. What does that lead to? To begin with, it must be said that decomposition into components is, in general, extremely important for any science. We have seen that up to now there has been no means of doing this completely objectively for the tale. This is a first, highly important conclusion. But furthermore, schemes may be compared, and then a whole series of those questions touched upon previously in the introductory chapter will be resolved. We shall now undertake the solution of these questions.

C. *The Problem of Classification*

We previously described the failure which befell the classification of the tale according to themes. Let us make use of our deductions for a classification according to structural features.

At this point two problems must be singled out: (1) the separation of the fairy tale class from other classes of tales; (2) the classification of fairy tales themselves.

The stability of construction of fairy tales permits a hypothetical *definition* of them which may be stated in the following way: a fairy tale is a story built upon the proper alternation of the above-cited functions in various forms, with some of them absent from each story and with others repeated. By such a definition the term "fairy" (*volšébnyj*) loses its sense, since it is a simple matter for one to imagine a wonderful, fantastic fairy tale constructed in a totally different way. (Compare certain of Andersen's and Brentano's tales, or Goethe's tale of the dragon and the lily, etc.) On the other hand, non-fairy tales may also be constructed according to the scheme cited. Quite a large number of legends, individual tales about animals, and isolated novellas display the same structure. The term "fairy," therefore, ought to be replaced by another. Finding such a term is very difficult, and we shall temporarily leave these tales with their old name. It may be changed in connection with the study of other classes, which will make possible the creation of a terminology. Fairy tales could be called tales subordinated to a seven-personage scheme. This term is highly exact but very awkward. If tales of this class are defined from a historical point of view, they then merit the antique, now discarded, name of mythical tales.

Of course, such a definition of this class requires a preliminary analysis. It should not be expected that the analysis of a particular text can be executed quickly and easily. Often an element which is unclear in one text is very clear in a parallel or different text. But whenever there is no parallel, the text remains unclear. The execution of a correct analysis of a tale is not always easy. A certain amount of experience and skill are required for this. It is true that many tales in the Russian collections can easily be decomposed. The job is complicated, however, by the fact that uncorrupted tale construction is peculiar only to the peasantry—to a peasantry, moreover, little touched by civilization. All kinds of foreign influences alter and sometimes even corrupt a tale. Complications begin as soon as we leave the boundary of the absolutely authentic tale. In this relation, the Afanás'ev collection is surprisingly gratifying material. But the tales of the Brothers Grimm, presenting the same scheme in general, display a less pure and stable form of it. It is impossible to provide for all the details. One must also keep in mind that just as elements are assimilated within a tale, whole *genres* are also assimilated and intermingled. Highly complicated conglomerates are then sometimes formed, into which the components of our scheme enter as episodes. It might also be pointed out that a similar construction is displayed by a number of very archaic myths, some of which present this structure in an amazingly pure form. Evidently this is the realm back to which the tale may be traced. On the other hand, the very same structure is exhibited, for example, by certain novels of chivalry. This is very likely a realm which itself may be traced back to the tale. A detailed comparative study is a task for the future.

In order to show that several tales about animals are also constructed in a similar manner, we shall examine the tale about the wolf and the kids (Af. No. 53). This tale furnishes us with an initial situation (the goat and the kids), the absence of an elder, an interdiction, the fraudulent persuasion of the villain (the wolf), the violation of the interdiction, the kidnapping of a member of the family, communication of the misfortune, a search, the slaying of the villain (a very interesting instance of an assimilation with difficult tasks: the goat proposes to the wolf that he jump over a pit; compare No. 137: the princess proposes to the tsar that he cross over a pit on a pole).† The slaying of the wolf simultaneously amounts to his punishment. The recovery of the kidnapped kids and their return follows. Thus this tale should be excluded from the class of tales about animals. It furnishes this scheme:

$$\gamma^1\beta^1\delta^1 A^1 B^4 C\uparrow I^6 K^1\downarrow$$

Thus, by employing structural features (*struktúrnye príznaki*), a given class may be discerned from others absolutely accurately and objectively.

Next we must separate tales in their essence. In order to guard against errors in logic, we shall note that a correct classification may be accomplished in a three-fold manner: (1) according to the varieties of *one* sign (deciduous or coniferous trees); (2) according to the absence or presence of one or another sign (vertebrates vs. invertebrates); (3) according to mutually exclusive signs (two-toed animals vs. rodents among mammals). Within the limits of one classification devices may change only according to genera, species, and varieties, or by other degrees of gradation, but each degree of gradation requires consistency, and uniformity of technique.

If one now were to glance at our schemes (which are cited a little further on), one might wonder whether it is not possible to make a classification according to mutually exclusive signs. At first glance it seems impossible, since not a single function excludes another. But on a more detailed examination, we observe that there are two such pairs of functions which are encountered within a single move so rarely that their exclusiveness

†". . . sr. No. 77: carevna predlagaet carju perejti po žerdočke čerez jamu" (p. 110). More accurately, in the tale cited (= new no. 137) it is the hero, Iván Bykovič, who makes this proposal to the old father of the *čudo-judas* (many-headed dragons), saying that whoever walks across on the pole will also take the tsarina for himself. [L.A.W.]

may be considered regular, while their combination may be considered a violation of the rule (this, however, as we shall later see, does not contradict our assertion concerning the typological unity of tales). These two pairs are the struggle with the villain and victory over him (H-I), and the difficult task and its resolution (M-N). In 100 tales the first pair is encountered 41 times, the second pair 33 times, and the two combined into one move three times. We further observe that moves exist which develop without these functions. Thus, four classes are immediately formed: development through H-I, development through M-N, development through both H-I and M-N, and development without either.

But the classification of tales is made extraordinarily complicated by the fact that many tales consist of several moves. At the moment we are speaking of one-move tales; for the present we shall continue to subdivide simple tales, returning later to the composite ones.

Further division may no longer proceed according to purely structural features, since only H-I and M-N are mutually exclusive, while none of the remaining functions are. Consequently, it is necessary to choose a single element which is obligatory for all tales and to make the division according to its varieties. A (villainy), or *a* (lack) are the only such obligatory elements. Further classification can be made according to the varieties of these elements. Thus at the head of each class will come the tales about the kidnapping of a person, then tales about the stealing of a talisman, etc., on through all the varieties of element A. Next will come tales with *a,* i.e. tales about the quest for a bride, for a talisman, etc. It is possible to object that in this way two tales with identical beginnings will fall into different classes depending on whether or not, for example, a difficult task is present in them. This will indeed occur, but it is not an objection to the correctness of our classification. Tales with H-I and those with M-N are essentially tales of different formation, since these features exclude one another. The presence or absence of the given element is their basic structural feature. In zoology, in exactly the same manner, the whale does not fall under the category of fishes, since it breathes by means of lungs, even though externally it looks very much like a fish. The eel, in the very same way, is classified in the category of fishes, even though it looks like a snake; the potato falls into the category of stems, though everyone takes it to be a root, and so on. This is a classification by structural, interior features, and not by features which are external and changeable.

Further, the question arises of what to do with tales of many moves, i.e., with tales in which we have several villainies, each of which develops separately.

There can be only one way out here: it should be stated, in reference to each multi-move text, that the first move is such and such, and that the second move is something else again. There is no other solution. This is perhaps clumsy and inconvenient, especially if one desires to compose a concise table of classification, but it is both logical and correct in essence.

Thus we apparently obtain four types of tales. Does this not contradict our assertion concerning the complete uniformity of all fairy tales? If elements H-I and M-N exclude one another in one move, does this not mean that we have two certain basic types of tales and not one, as we asserted previously? No, this is not so. If we carefully examine those tales which consist of two moves, we will observe the following: if one move contains a fight and the other a difficult task, then the fight always occurs in the first move and the difficult task in the second. These tales give a typical beginning for second moves, namely, the casting of Iván into a chasm by his brothers, and so on. For such tales a two-move structure is canonical. This is *one* tale consisting of two moves, the basic type of all tales. It is easily separated into two parts. The brothers introduce the complication. If brothers were not introduced at the very beginning, or if their role were in general limited, then the tale might conclude with Iván's happy return (i.e., with the end of the first move), and the second move would not need to follow. In this manner the first half can exist as an independent tale. On the other hand, the second half is also a finished tale. By substituting the brothers with other villains or by simply beginning with the quest for the bride, we have a tale which can cause development via difficult tasks. Thus each move may exist separately, but only a combination of the two moves produces an entirely complete tale. It is quite possible that two types existed historically, that each has its own history, and that in some remote epoch the two traditions met and merged into one formation. But in speaking about Russian fairy tales we are compelled to say that today this is one tale, to which all the tales of our class are traced.

D. *On the Relationship of Particular Forms of Structure to the General Pattern*

Let us examine the nature of each aspect of our tales.

1. If we add up, one under the other, all schemes which include struggle-victory and also those instances in which we have a simple killing of the enemy without a fight, we will obtain the following scheme: [2]

ABC↑DEFGHJIK↓Pr Rs° LQ Ex TUW *.

2. If we add up, one under the other, all schemes including difficult tasks, we obtain the following result:

ABC↑DEFG° LMJNK↓Pr Rs Q Ex TUW *.

A comparison of the two resultant schemes gives the following results:

ABC↑DEFG HJIK↓Pr Rs° LQ Ex TUW *.
ABC↑DEFG° LMJNK↓Pr Rs Q Ex TUW *.

It is evident from this that struggle-victory (H-I) and difficult tasks and their resolution (M-N) correspond to one another with respect to their position in the series of other functions. Among these functions places are shifted only by the unrecognized arrival and by the demand of the false hero (°-L) which follow the fight but precede the difficult tasks (i.e., the prince in the guise of a cook, the water carrier pretends to be the victor; Iván takes up residence at home with an artisan, the brothers pass themselves off as obtainers of the spoils).

Further, it can be observed that moves with difficult tasks are most often second, repeated, or singular moves, and very rarely (only once) occur first. If a tale consists of two moves, then moves containing a fight always precede those involving tasks. Hence we conclude that a move with H-I is a typical first move, and a move with difficult tasks is a typical second or repeated move. Each of them is also capable of existing separately, but a combination always takes place in the order named. Theoretically, of course, the reverse combination is also possible; but in such cases we shall always be faced with a mechanical combination of two tales.

3. Tales which include both pairs present the following picture: [3]

$$ABC\uparrow FH\text{-}IK\downarrow LM\text{-}NQ\ Ex\ UW\ *.$$

Here functions H-I are also seen to precede functions M-N. Function L stands between them.

The three cases studied do not give material for an opinion as to whether pursuit is possible in the given combination. It is absent in all instances which have been examined.

4. If all schemes which do not contain either struggle in any of its forms or difficult tasks are added one after another, the following will result:

$$ABC\uparrow DEFGK\downarrow Pr\ Rs\ Q\ Ex\ TUW\ *$$

If the scheme of these tales is compared with the foregoing schemes it is apparent that these tales also do not present any specific construction. To the variable scheme

$$ABC\uparrow DEFG\frac{HJIK\downarrow Pr\text{-}Rs^{\circ}\ L}{LMJNK\downarrow Pr\text{-}Rs}Q\ Ex\ TUW\ *$$

are subject all tales of our material: moves with H-I develop according to the upper branch; moves with M-N develop according to the lower branch; moves with both pairs first follow the upper part and then, without coming to an end, develop following the lower offshoot; moves without either H-I or M-N develop by bypassing the distinctive elements of each.

Let us compile our material according to this scheme. For greater clarity let us write out the resultant scheme first on one line. Elements H-I and M-N, being incompatible, are written out one under the other.[4] (The schemes have been transferred to Appendix III.)

What conclusions does this scheme present? In the first place, it affirms our general thesis regarding the total uniformity in the construction of fairy tales.

This most important general conclusion at first does not coincide with our conception of the richness and variety of tales.

As has already been indicated, this conclusion appeared quite unexpectedly. It was an unexpected one for the author of this work as well. This phenomenon is so unusual and strange that one somehow feels a desire to dwell upon it, prior to going on to more particular, formal conclusions. Naturally, it is not our business to interpret this phenomenon; our job is only to state the fact itself. Yet one still feels inclined to pose this question: if all fairy tales are so similar in form, does this not mean that they all originate from a single source? The morphologist does not have the right to answer this question. At this point he hands over his conclusions to a historian or should himself become a historian. Our answer, although in the form of a supposition, is that this appears to be so. However, the question of sources should not be posed merely in a narrowly geographic sense. "A single source" does not positively signify, as some assume, that all tales came, for example, from India, and that they spread from there throughout the entire world, assuming various forms in the process of their migration. The single source may also be a psychological one. Much has been done by Wundt in this sphere. But here also one must be very cautious. If the limitation of the tale were to be explained by the limited faculties of human imagination in general, we would have no tales other than those of our given category, but we possess thousands of other tales not resembling fairy tales. Finally, this single source may come from everyday life. But a morphological study of the tale will show that it contains very little pertaining to everyday life. Certain transitional stages from the pattern of daily living to tales do exist, and this pattern is indirectly reflected in them. One such transitional stage is found in beliefs which arose at a certain stage in the development of daily life, and it is very possible that there is a natural connection between everyday life and religion, on the one hand, and between religion and the tale on the other. A way of life and religion die out, while their contents turn into tales. As indicated previously, tales contain such obvious traces of religious notions that they can be tracked down without the help of a historical study. But since such a supposition is more easily clarified historically, we shall cite a small illustrative parallel between tales and beliefs. The tale evidences three basic forms of Iván's bearers through the air. These are the flying steed, the bird, and the flying boat. But it happens that these forms represent bearers of the souls of the departed, with the horse predominating among agricultural and herding peoples, the eagle prevailing among hunters, and the boat predominant among inhabitants of the seacoast.[5] Frobenius even cites the representation of such a ship for souls (*Seelenschiff*) from Northwest America. Thus one may suppose that one of the basic elements of tale composition, i.e., *wandering,* reflects notions about the wandering of souls in the other world. This notion, together with certain others, could undoubtedly have arisen independently of one another throughout the entire globe. Cultural crossings and the dying out of beliefs complete the rest. The flying steed gives way to the more amusing carpet. But we have gone too far astray. We shall leave this to be judged by the historian. The tale has still been studied very little on the plane of its parallel with religion and its further penetration into the cultural and economic aspects of daily living.

This is the most general, fundamental deduction of our entire work. It is no longer possible to say, along with Speránskij, that no generalizations exist in the study of the tale. It is true that the present generalization is only an attempt. But if it is correct, it should in the future bring after it a series of other general conclusions. Perhaps then the secret in which the tale is still so deeply wrapped will gradually begin to unfold.

Let us, however, return to our scheme. The assertion concerning absolute stability would seem to be unconfirmed by the fact that the sequence of functions is not always the same as that shown in the total scheme. A careful examination of the schemes will show certain deviations. In particular, one may observe that elements DEF often stand before A. Does this not break the rule? No, for this is not a new, but rather an *inverted* (*obraščënnyj*) sequence.

The usual tale presents, for example, a misfortune at first and then the receipt of a helper who liquidates it. An inverted sequence gives the receipt of a helper at first and then the misfortune which is liquidated by him (elements DEF before A). Another example: misfortune is usually given first, followed by the exit from home (ABC↑). An inverted sequence first provides the exit from home, which is usually aimless ("to have a look at people and to show oneself," etc.); then when the hero is already on the road he learns of the misfortune.

Some functions are capable of changing places. In tales 93 and 159 the fight with the villain takes place only after pursuit.

Recognition and exposure, marriage and punishment may also exchange positions. Among individual functions, the transference of a magical agent sometimes occurs before the hero leaves home. These are the cudgels, ropes, maces, and so forth, given by the father. A transference of this type is most often encountered in the case of agrarian plunderings (A^8), but it can also be found in connection with other complications and in no way predetermines the possibility or impossibility of an encounter with a donor of the usual type. The most unstable function in relation to its position is T (transfiguration). Logically, its most appropriate position is either before or after the punishment of the false hero, or else before the wedding, where it is indeed most often encountered. All of these deviations do not alter the deduction concerning the typological unity and morphological kinship of fairy tales. These are only fluctuations and not a new compositional system or new axes. There are certain cases, as well, of direct violations. In isolated tales the violations are rather significant (164, 248), but a closer examination will reveal these to be humorous tales. A transposition of this kind, accompanying the transformation of a poem into a farce, must be recognized as the result of dissolution.

Isolated tales present an incomplete form in relation to the basic type. One or another function is absent in all tales. If a function is absent, this does not in the least influence the structure of the tale—the remaining functions keep their places. Often it is possible to show, according to certain rudiments, that this absence amounts to an omission.

The functions of the preparatory section are also wholly subject to these conclusions. If we were to write out all instances in our material, one under another, the sum would in general show the same sequence cited previously in the enumeration of functions. However, the study of this section is complicated by the following circumstance: all seven functions of this section are never encountered within one tale, and an absence here can never be explained as omission. They essentially are incompatible. One may observe here that one and the same phenomenon is capable of being elicited by several means. For example, in order that the villain may create misfortune, the storyteller has to place the hero or the victim in a certain state of helplessness. Most often he must be parted from his parents, elders, or protectors. This is brought about by the hero's violation of an interdiction (he leaves home, in spite of a prohibition to do so); or the hero goes out for a walk on his own, etc. (β^3); or it is achieved by the fact that the hero yields to the deception of the villain who invites him to walk toward the sea or who lures him into the forest, etc. Thus if the tale makes use of one of the pairs γ-δ (interdiction-violation), or η-θ (deception-submission to deception) for this end, the use of a second pair is often unnecessary. Frequently the transmission of information to the villain may also be achieved by the hero's violation of an interdiction. Therefore if *several* pairs are employed in the preparatory section, one can always expect a double morphological meaning (in violating the interdiction, the hero gives himself up to the villain, etc.) A detailed clarification of this question requires additional analysis based upon a larger amount of material.

A most important question which may be further posed in examining the schemes is the following: are the varieties of one function necessarily linked with the corresponding varieties of another function? The schemes answer this question in the following way:

1. There are elements which, without exception, are *always* linked with varieties corresponding to one another. These are certain pairs within the limits of their halves. Thus H^1 (fight in an open field), is always connected with I^1 (victory in an open field), and a connection with, for example, I^3 (winning at cards) is completely impossible and devoid of sense. All varieties of the following pairs are permanently joined to one another: interdiction and its violation; the attempt to find out something and the transmission of information; deception (fraud) by the villain and the hero's reaction to it; fight and victory; marking and recognition.

Besides these pairs in which *all* varieties are permanently connected only to one another, there exist pairs about which one may say the same thing in regard to *several* varieties. Thus, within the confines of villainy and its liquidation, we have a stable connection between murder and resuscitation, enchantment and the breaking of a spell, and several others. In regard to the varieties of pursuit and rescue, pursuit accompanied by rapid transformations into animals is always connected with a corresponding form of rescue. In this manner we find established the presence of certain elements whose varieties are stably connected to one another on the strength of logical and at times also artistic necessity.

2. Pairs exist in which one half may be connected with certain but not all varieties of its corresponding half. Kidnapping may be linked with a direct counter-kidnapping (K^1); with a recovery via two or more helpers (K^1, K^2); with a recovery via an instantaneous return of a magical nature (K^5), etc. In exactly the same way, direct pursuit may be linked with rescue by means of a simple flight, with rescue by means of fleeing and throwing down a comb, with a transformation of the pursued person into a church or a well, with the concealment of the pursued person, and so forth. However, it is easy to observe that one function within the limits of a pair can often provoke several responses, but each of these responses is bound only to the particular form which calls it forth. Thus the throwing of the comb is always linked with direct pursuit, whereas direct pursuit is not always connected with the throwing of a comb. In this light, there appear to exist elements which are capable of unilateral and bilateral substitution. We shall not dwell on this difference at present. We only point out elements D and F, examined previously in the third chapter, as examples capable of very broad bilateral substitution.

It is necessary, however, to make note of the fact that these norms of dependence, as obvious as they are in themselves, are sometimes violated by the tale. Villainy and its liquidation (A-K) are separated from each other by a long story. In the course of the tales the narrator loses the thread of the story, and one may observe that element K sometimes does not quite correspond to the initial A or *a*. The tale is as though out of tune. Iván sets out after a steed but returns with a princess. This phenomenon is valuable material for the study of transformations: the storyteller has either changed the exposition or the dénouement, and from similar comparisons certain methods of change and substitution can be deduced. We have a phenomenon similar to "disharmony" when the first half does not evoke the usual response, or else replaces it with a response that is completely different and unusual for the tale norm. In tale No. 260 the enchantment of a boy is not followed by any breaking of the spell, and he remains a little goat for life. "The Wonderful

Fife" (No. 244) is a very interesting tale. Here, murder is not nullified by the resuscitation of the victim. Resuscitation is replaced by the disclosure of the murder, and the form of this disclosure amounts to an assimilation with B^7: it is presented in the form of a lament on which the tale ends, adding only the punishment of the sister-murderess. In connection with this instance it can be observed that *banishment* has no specific form for its liquidation. It is simply replaced by a return. Banishment is often a false villainy, motivating↑. The hero does not return at all, but gets married, and so forth.

3. All remaining elements, including actual pairs, can be freely connected without any violation of logic or artistic values. It is easy to see that in a given tale the abduction of a person does not require that the following of bloody tracks be replaced by either flight or indication of the way. Similarly, in the capture of a talisman there is no reason to compel the hero to subject himself to persecution by an attempted murder rather than by pursuit through the air. Thus the principle of complete freedom and mutual substitution is dominant here. In this respect these elements are diametrically opposed to those elements like H-I, which are always and necessarily bound to one another. We are speaking exclusively of this *principle*. However, people make little use of this freedom, and the number of actually existent connections is not very great. Thus, no tales exist in which enchantment is connected with a call, even though this is both artistically and logically quite possible. Nonetheless, the establishment of this principle of freedom, alongside that of the lack of freedom, is very important. The variation of themes and the metamorphosis of tales are carried out by the substitution of one form by the same element of another form.

These conclusions, moverover, may also be verified experimentally. It is possible to artificially create new plots of an unlimited number. All of these plots will reflect the basic scheme, while they themselves may not resemble one another. In order to create a tale artificially, one may take any A, then one of the possible B's then a C↑, followed by absolutely any D, then an E, then one of the possible F's, then any G, and so on. In doing this, any elements may be dropped (except possibly for A or *a*), or repeated three times, or repeated in various forms. If one then distributes functions according to the dramatis personae of the tale's supply or by following one's own taste, these schemes come alive and become tales.[6] Of course, one must also keep motivations, connections, and other auxiliary elements in mind. The application of these conclusions to folk creation naturally requires great caution. The psychology of the storyteller and the psychology of his creative work as a part of the over-all psychology of creation must be studied independently. But it is possible to assume that the basic, vivid moments of our essentially very simple scheme also play the psychological role of a kind of root. But then new tales will always appear merely as combinations or variations of older ones. This seems to say that there is no creation on the part of the people in regard to the tale. This is not quite so, however. It is possible to accurately demarcate those areas in which the folk narrator never creates, and areas in which he creates more or less freely. The storyteller is constrained and does not create in the following areas: (1) In the over-all sequence of functions, the series of which develops according to the above indicated scheme. This phenomenon presents a complicated problem which we cannot explain here; we can only state the fact. It ought to be studied by anthropology and the contiguous disciplines which alone are capable of shedding light on its causes. (2) The storyteller is not at liberty to make substitutions for those elements whose varieties are connected by an absolute or relative dependence. (3) In other instances, the storyteller is not free to select certain personages on the basis of their attributes in the event that a definite function is required. It must be said, however, that this lack of freedom is highly relative. Thus, if function G^1 (flight) is required, the Water of Life cannot figure in the capacity of a magical gift, whereas a steed, a carpet, a ring (young men), or a little box, as well as very many others, can function here. (4) A certain dependence exists between the initial situation and the functions which follow it. In the event of a required or desired use of function A^2 (the kidnapping of a helper), this helper must be included in the situation. The storyteller is free, on the other hand, to create in the following areas: (1) In the choice of those functions which he omits or, conversely, which he uses. (2) In the choice of the means (form) through which a function is realized. As has already been pointed out, the formation of new variants, new plots, and new tales takes place in just this way. (3) The storyteller is completely free in his choice of the nomenclature and attributes of the dramatis personae. Theoretically, the freedom here is absolute. A tree may show the way, a crane may give a steed as a gift, a chisel may spy, etc. This freedom is a specific peculiarity of the tale alone. It must be said, however, that here too, people do not make very wide use of this freedom. Personages recur just as functions do. Here, as previously indicated, a special canon has evolved (the dragon is the typical villain, the witch is the typical donor, Iván is the typical seeker, and so on). The canon changes but these changes are very rarely the product of personal artistic creation. It can be established that the creator of a tale rarely invents; he receives his material from his surroundings or from current realities and adapts them to a tale.[7] (4) The storyteller is free in his choice of linguistic means. This highly rich area is not subject to the morphologist's study. The *style* of a tale is a phenomenon which must be studied separately.

E. *The Problem of Composition and Theme, and of Themes and Variants*

Up to now we have examined the tale exclusively from the viewpoint of its structure. We observed that in the past it was always examined from the point of view of theme, and we cannot pass this question by. But since no single, generally accepted, interpretation of the word "theme" (*sjužét*) exists, we have carte blanche and may define this concept in our own way.

The entire contents of a tale may be stated in brief phrases such as the following: parents leave for the forest; they forbid their children to go out into the street; a dragon kidnaps the little girl, and so forth. All *predicates* give the composition of tales; all *subjects, objects,* and other parts of the sentence define the theme. In other words, the same composition may lie at the base of various themes. From the point of view of composition, it does not matter whether a dragon kidnaps a princess or whether a devil makes off with either a priest's or a peasant's daughter. But these cases may be examined as different themes. We also admit other definitions of the concept of theme, but the given definition is suitable for fairy tales.

How shall we distinguish a theme from a variant? If we have, let us say, a tale of the form A^1 B^1 C D^1 E^1 F^1, etc., and a second one of the form A^1 B^2 C D^1 E^1 F^1, etc., the question is whether the alteration of one element (B), while retaining all of the others, creates a new theme or only a variant of the former one. It is clear that this is a variant. And what if two, three, or four elements are altered, or one, two, or three elements are either omitted or added? The question is changed from one of quality to one of quantity. Regardless of how we might have defined the concept of theme, the distinction between theme and variant is totally impossible. Here there can be only two points of view. Either each alteration gives a new theme, or all tales provide one theme in diverse variants. As a matter of fact, both formulations express the same thing: the entire store of fairy tales ought to be examined as a *chain* of variants. Were we able to unfold the picture of transformations, it would be possible to satisfy ourselves that all of the tales given can be morphologically deduced from the tales about the kidnapping of a princess by a dragon—from that form which we are inclined to consider as basic. This is a very bold assertion, especially since we do not present the picture of transformations in this work. It would be important in this case to have very extensive material. Tales could be arranged so that a picture of the gradual transition from one theme to another would turn out to be quite clear. Of course, certain jumps and gaps would result here and there. People do not present all of the mathematically possible forms. But this does not contradict the hypothesis. Let us remember that tales have been collected for no more than a hundred years. They began to be collected in an era when they had already begun to disintegrate. There are no new formations at present. But there undoubtedly were exceptionally productive, creative epochs. Aarne considers that the Middle Ages was such an era in Europe. The contemporary absence of certain forms will not contradict the over-all theory if one realizes that those centuries in which the tale led an intense existence are irretrievably lost to science. Just as we conjecture on the basis of general astronomical laws about the existence of those stars which we cannot see, it is also possible to assume the existence of tales which have not been collected.

From this there follows a very important application of a methodological nature.

If our observations about the exceptionally close morphological kinship of tales are correct, it follows that no single theme of a given genus of tales may be studied either morphologically or genetically without reference to others. One theme changes into another by means of the substitution of elements according to forms. Naturally, the task of studying some individual tale in all of its variants and according to its total dissemination is very tempting. But this task is, in essence, incorrectly stated. If, for example, in such a tale a magical steed, or grateful animals, or a wise woman, etc., are encountered, and the investigation deals with them only in the given combination, it may happen that not a single element of the given combination will be studied exhaustively. The conclusions of such a study will be shaky and incorrect, since each element may also be encountered in another application and may have its own history.

All of these elements should first be studied in themselves, independently of their use in this or that tale. Now, when the folk tale is still full of mysteries for us, we first of all need to have an elucidation of each element separately throughout the entire tale material. Miraculous birth, interdictions, rewarding with magical agents, flight and pursuit, etc., are all elements which merit independent monographs. It goes without saying that such study cannot limit itself solely to the tale. The majority of its elements are traceable to one or another archaic cultural, religious, daily, or other reality which must be utilized for comparison. Following the study of separate elements, there must be a genetic study of the axis on which all fairy tales are formed. Certainly the norms and forms of metamorphoses must be studied. Only after this can one proceed to the study of the question of how separate themes were formed, and what they represent.

F. *Conclusion*

With our work finished, it remains for us to supply a conclusion. There is no point in summarizing the theses. They are placed at the beginning, and the entire work is imbued with them. In place of this we may state that our propositions, although they appear to be new, were intuitively foreseen by none other than Veselóvskij, and it is with his words that we end this study:

Is it permissible in this field also to consider the problem of typical schemes . . . schemes handed down for generations as ready-made formulae capable of becoming animated with a new mood, giving rise to new formations? . . . Contemporary narrative literature, with its complicated thematic structure and photographic reproduction of reality apparently eliminates the very possibility of such a question. But when this literature will appear to future generations as distant as antiquity, from prehistoric to medieval times, seems to us at present—when the synthesis of time, that great simplifier, in passing over the complexity of phenomena, reduces them to the magnitude of points receding into the distance, then their lines will merge with those which we are now uncovering when we look back at the poetic traditions of the distant past—and the phenomena of schematism and repetition will then be established across the total expanse.[8]

NOTES

1. The numbers given in parentheses refer to tables in Appendix I.

2. A scheme without the functions of the preparatory section; these are treated further on.

3. The three instances in our material are 123, 136 (IV), and 136 (IV), and 171 (III). [For an analysis of tale 123, see Appendix II; for a remark on the fourth move of tale 136, see the "Commentary to Individual Schemes" in Appendix III. (L.A.W.].

4. For technical reasons trebling cannot be shown here. If functions, or a group of them, are repeated in various aspects, such a repetition is designated by the addition of repetitive elements, one under another. Interweaving moves are separated and each is recorded separately, while the interruption of a move is designated by dots, together with an indication of just which move breaks the thread. A lack, if it is not underscored by a tale (the hero is not married, for example), is put into brackets. Functions of the preparatory section were not included in the scheme due to lack of space. We shall speak separately about them later on. The Arabic numerals indicate the enumeration of tales according to the collection of Afanás'ev. The Roman numerals are the moves according to the data of our analysis. All explanations of individual schemes follow the transcriptions in Appendix III. The negative result of a function is designated by a hyphen (minus sign). Therefore F— indicates that nothing is given to the hero. The form F contr. is designated as F=.

5. Cf. J. V. Negelein, "Die Reise der Seele ins Jenseits," *Zeitschrift d. Vereins für Volkskunde, 1901–02;* also his "Das Pferd im Seelenglauben und Totenkult," *ibid;* Weicker, *Der Seelenvogel;* L. Frobenius, *Die Weltanschauung der Naturvölker,* especially Chapter I, "Die Vogelmythe," etc.

6. Cf. Šklóvskij: "The tale is collected and laid out according to laws still unknown." This law has been determined.

7. At this point the following proposition may be stated: everything drawn into a tale from outside is subject to its norms and laws. A devil, on being taken into the tale, is treated either as a villain, a helper, or a donor. This proposition works especially interestingly on archaic material from daily life and other areas. Thus, among certain peoples the reception of a new member into tribal society

is accomplished by the placing of bloody marks on his forehead, cheeks, and shoulders (Lippert, *Istorija kul'tury v otdel'nyx očerkax,* p. 213). We easily recognize the marking of the hero before marriage. The placing of a brand on his shoulders has not been retained since our shoulders are now covered by clothing. Marking of the forehead and cheeks remains and is often bloody, but employed exclusively for artistic purposes.

8. A. N. Veselovskij, *Poètika* (Poetics), Vol. II, fasc. 1 ("Poètika sjužetov"), Chapter 1.

APPENDIX I

MATERIALS FOR A TABULATION OF THE TALE

Since we were able to examine only the functions of the dramatis personae and were obligated to set aside all other elements, we offer here a list of all the elements of the fairy tale. Although the list does not completely exhaust the content of each tale, the majority of tales fit into it entirely. If one imagines the tale given below as laid out on a single sheet, a horizontal reading will not always present the sequence which is present in a tale. This would be possible only with respect to the functions as a whole. Moreover, there is no need to do this. In setting down each text in detail under a given heading, each heading (when the material is read vertically) offers an extremely graphic picture and may be studied entirely independently. The texts which have been set down may be distributed in such a way as to emphasize the specially typical forms. A comparison of the material under each heading makes possible the study of the transformation and metamorphosis of each element. This study could be made even broader and more exact if there were added to each item a designation of its present custodian, and also of the time and place of recording.

TABLE I: *The Initial Situation*

1. Temporal-spatial determination ("in a certain kingdom").
2. Composition of the family:
    a. according to nomenclature and status;
    b. according to the categories of dramatis personae (dispatcher, seeker, etc.).
3. Childlessness.

4–5. Prayer for the birth of a son:
  4. form of the prayer;
  5. motivation of the prayer.

6. Cause of pregnancy:
  a. intentional (a fish which is eaten, etc.);
  b. accidental (a swallowed pea, etc.);
  c. forced (a girl is abducted by a bear, etc.).

7. Form of miraculous birth:
  a. from a fish and from water;
  b. from a hearth;
  c. from an animal;
  d. otherwise.

8. Prophecies, forewarnings.

9. Well-being, prior to complication (*zavjázka*):
  a. fantastic;
  b. domestic;
  c. agrarian;
  d. in other forms.

10–15. The future hero:
  10. nomenclature, sex;
  11. rapid growth;
  12. connection with a hearth, ashes;
  13. spiritual qualities;
  14. michievousness;
  15. other qualities.

16–20. The future false hero (of the first type: a brother, a stepsister):
  16. nomenclature, sex;
  17. degree of kinship to the hero;
  18. negative qualities;
  19. spiritual qualities in comparison with the hero (clever);
  20. other qualities.

21–23. Argument of brothers over primacy:
  21. form of the argument and manner of solution;
  22. auxiliary elements trebled;
  23. result of the argument.

TABLE II: *The Preparatory Section*

24–26. Interdictions:
- 24. person performing;
- 25. contents, form of the interdiction;
- 26. motivation of the interdiction.

27–29. Absentations:
- 27. person performing;
- 28. form of absentation;
- 29. motivation of absentation.

30–32. Violation of an interdiction:
- 30. person performing;
- 31. form of violation;
- 32. motivation.

33–35. First appearance of the villain:
- 33. nomenclature;
- 34. manner of inclusion into the course of action (appears from outside);
- 35. details of external appearance on the scene (flies in through the ceiling).

36–38. Interrogation, reconnaissance:
- 36. what motivates it;
- 37. nature of the interrogation:
  - a. the villain asks about the hero;
  - b. the hero asks about the villain;
  - c. otherwise;
- 38. auxiliary elements trebled.

39.†

40–42. Delivery:
- 40. person betraying;
- 41. forms of response to the villain (or a careless act):
  - a. forms of response to the hero;
  - b. other forms of response;
  - c. delivery through careless acts;
- 42. auxiliary elements trebled.

†In the original text, number 39 is missing (or else there is an error in enumeration). [L.A.W.]

43. The villain's deceptions:
    a. through persuasions;
    b. through use of magical means;
    c. otherwise.

44. Preliminary misfortune in a deceptive agreement:
    a. misfortune is present;
    b. misfortune provoked by the villain himself.

45. Reaction of the hero:
    a. to persuasions;
    b. to the use of magical agents;
    c. to other acts of the villain.

TABLE III: *The Complication* (zavjázka)

46–51. Villainy:
- 46. person performing;
- 47. form of villainy (or designation of lack);
- 48. object of the villain's influence (or object of lack);
- 49. owner of object or father of person captured (or person realizing lack, lacks, or motivation of dispatch);
- 50. motivation and aim of villainy (or form of realization);
- 51. forms of the villain's disappearance. Examples: (46) a dragon (47) kidnaps (48) the daughter (49) of the tsar (50) with the intent of forced matrimony (51) and flies away. In the case of lacks: (46–47) lacking, missing, or needed is (48) the deer with golden antlers (49) for the tsar (50) in order to destroy the hero.

52–57. The conjunctive moment (B):
- 52. personage—intermediary, dispatcher;
- 53. form of mediation;
- 54. person to whom it is addressed;
- 55. for what end;
- 56. auxiliary elements trebled;
- 57. how the intermediary learns of the hero (§).

58–60. The seeker's or hero's entry into the tale:
- 58. nomenclature;
- 59. form of inclusion into the course of the action;
- 60. external peculiarities of appearance on the scene.

61. Form of the hero's consent.

62. Form of dispatch of the hero.

63–66. Phenomena accompanying him:
- 63. threats;
- 64. promises;
- 65. equipping for the journey;
- 66. auxiliary elements trebled.

67. Dispatch of the hero from home.

68–69. Goal of the hero:
- 68. goal as an action (to seek out, to liberate, to rescue);
- 69. goal as an object (a princess, a magical steed, etc.).

TABLE IV: *Donors*

70. Journey from home to the donor.

71–77. Donors:
- 71. manner of inclusion into the tale, nomenclature;
- 72. dwelling;
- 73. physical appearance;
- 74. peculiarities of external appearance on the scene;
- 75. other attributes;
- 76. dialogue with the hero;
- 77. hospitality shown to the hero.

78. Preparation for the transmission of a magical agent:
- a. tasks;
- b. requests;
- c. skirmish;
- d. other forms; trebling.

79. Reaction of the hero:
- a. positive;
- b. negative.

80–81. Provision:
- 80. what is given;
- 81. in what form.

TABLE V: *From the Entry of the Helper to the End of the First Move*

82–89. The helper (magical agent):
- 82. nomenclature;
- 83. form of summons;
- 84. manner of inclusion into the course of the action;
- 85. peculiarities of appearance on the scene;
- 86. physical appearance;
- 87. original location;
- 88. training (taming) of the helper;
- 89. wisdom of the helper.

90. Delivery to the appointed place.

91. Forms of arrival.

92. Details of the setting of the object sought for:
- a. dwelling of the princess;
- b. dwelling of the villain;
- c. description of the faraway kingdom.

93–97. Second appearance of the villain:
- 93. manner of inclusion into the course of the action (he is sought out, etc.);
- 94. physical appearance of the villain;
- 95. retinue;
- 96. peculiarities of external appearance on the scene;
- 97. dialogue of the villain with the hero.

98–101. Second (first, in the case of lacks) appearance of the princess (of the object of the quest):
- 98. manner of inclusion into the course of action;
- 99. physical appearance;
- 100. peculiarities of external appearance at the scene (she sits on the seashore, etc.);
- 101. dialogue.

102–105. Struggle with the villain:
- 102. place of the fight;
- 103. actions preceding the fight (clearing the field);
- 104. forms of the fight or struggle;
- 105. after the fight (cremation).

106–107. Marking:
- 106. personage;
- 107. manner.

108–109. Victory over the villain:
- 108. role of the hero;
- 109. role of the helper; trebling.

110–113. The false hero (of second type—water-carrier, general):
- 110. nomenclature;
- 111. forms of appearance on the scene;
- 112. behavior during battle;
- 113. dialogue with the princess, deceptions, etc.

114–119. Liquidation of misfortune or lack:
- 114. interdiction of the helper;
- 115. violation of the interdiction;
- 116. role of the hero;
- 117. role of the helper;
- 118. means;
- 119. auxiliary elements trebled.

120. Return.

121–124. Pursuit:
- 121. forms of notifying the villain about the escape;
- 122. forms of pursuit;
- 123. notification of hero about the pursuit;
- 124. auxiliary elements trebled.

125–127. Rescue from pursuit:
- 125. the rescuer;
- 126. forms;
- 127. downfall of the villain.

TABLE VI: *Beginning of the Second Move*

From a new villainy (A^1 or A^2, etc.) to the arrival—repetition of the preceding; same headings.

TABLE VII: *Continuation of the Second Move*

128. Unrecognized arrival:
    a. home, with entry into service;
    b. home, without entry into service;
    c. to another tsar's domain:
    d. other forms of concealment, etc.

129–131. Unfounded claims of the false hero:
    129. person performing;
    130. forms of claims;
    131. preparations for marriage.

132–136. The difficult task:
    132. the person who sets it;
    133. motivation for the task by the person who sets it (illness, etc.);
    134. actual motivation for the task (the desire to differentiate the false hero from the true one, etc.);
    135. contents of task;
    136. auxiliary elements trebled.

137–140. Resolution of the task:
    137. dialogue with the helper;
    138. role of the helper;
    139. form of solution;
    140. auxiliary elements trebled.

141–143. Recognition:
    141. means of summoning the true hero (spreading out a feast, making the rounds of beggars);
    142. form of the hero's appearance on the scene (at the wedding, etc.);
    143. form of recognition.

144–146. Exposure:
    144. person exposing;
    145. manner of exposing;
    146. motivation of exposure.

147–148. Transfiguration:
- 147. personage;
- 148. manner of transfiguration.

149–150. Punishment:
- 149. personage;
- 150. manner of punishment.

151. Wedding.

APPENDIX II

FURTHER TECHNIQUES OF ANALYSES

1. Analysis of a simple, single-move tale of class H-I, of the type: kidnapping of a person.

131. A tsar, three daughters (α). The daughters go walking (β^3), overstay in the garden (δ^1). A dragon kidnaps them (A^1). A call for aid (B^1). Quest of three heroes ($C\uparrow$). Three battles with the dragon (H^1-I^1), rescue of the maidens (K^4). Return ($\downarrow$), reward (w°).

$$\beta^3\delta^1A^1B^1C\uparrow H^1\text{-}I^1K^4\downarrow w^\circ$$

2. Analysis of a simple single-move tale of class M-N of the type: expulsion by water, coming ashore (A^{10}).

247. Merchant, wife, and son (α). A nightingale foretells the humiliation of the parents by the son. (Prophesy. Table I, No. 8. This serves as the motivation for the villainy.) The parents place the sleeping boy in a boat and set it adrift ($A^{10}\uparrow$). Boatmen take him with them (G^2). They arrive at Xvalýnsk (substitute for a faraway kingdom). The tsar sets the following task: to guess what the ravens cry in the royal courtyard and to drive them off (M). The boy resolves the task (N), marries the tsar's daughter (W^*), travels home ($\downarrow$); en route he recognizes his parents at an overnight lodging place (recognition).

$$\eta^3A^{10}\uparrow G^2M\text{-}N\ W^*\downarrow Q$$

Remark: The little boy fulfills the task because he has known the language of the birds from birth. Here element F^1 is dropped out—the transmission of a magical property. Consequently, the helper is also absent, and his attributes (wisdom) are transferred to the hero. The tale has preserved the rudiment of this helper: the nightingale which has foretold the humiliation of the parents flies away with the little boy and alights upon his shoulder. However, he does not take part in the course of the action. En route, the boy gives proof of his wisdom by foretelling a storm and the approach of robbers, thereby saving the boatman. This is an attribute of wisdom with auxiliary epic development.

3. Analysis of a simple single-move tale without H-I and M-N, of the type: murder.

244. A priest, his wife, his son Ivánuška, and daughter Alënuška (α). Alënuška goes out into the woods for berries (β^3, absentation). Her mother orders her to take her brother along with her (γ^2, order). Ivánuška gathers more berries than Alënuška (motivation for the villainy). "Let me look for lice in your hair" (persuasions of the villain [η^1]). Ivánuška falls asleep (θ^1). Alënuška kills her brother (A^{14}, murder). A thin reed grows upon the grave (appearance of a magical agent out of the ground [F^{vi}]). A shepherd plucks it and makes a pipe out of it (§). The pipe plays and reveals the murderess (exposure). The song is repeated five times, in different situations. It is actually a lament (B^7) which has been assimilated with exposure. The parents expel the daughter (punishment).

$$\gamma^2\beta^3\delta^2\eta^1\theta^1A^{14}F^{vi}[Ex]^5U$$

4. Analysis of a double-move tale with one villainy. Class H-I, type: kidnapping of a person.

133. I. A man, his wife, two sons, a daughter (α). The brothers, on leaving for work, request their sister to bring lunch to them ($\beta^1\gamma^2$); they show the road to the field with shavings (thereby betraying their sister to the dragon ζ^1). The dragon rearranges the shavings (η^3), the girl goes out to the field with the lunch (δ^2), and follows the wrong road (θ^3). The dragon kidnaps her (A^1). The brothers' quests (C↑). Herdsmen say: "Eat up my biggest ox" (D^1). The brothers are unable to do so (E^1 neg.). The dragon says: "Eat up twelve oxen," etc. (D^1), E^1 neg. follows. The brothers are thrown beneath a stone (F contr.).

II. Pokatigoróšek is born. The mother tells of the misfortune (B^4). Quests (C↑). Herdsmen and dragon—as before (D^1E^1, testing remains without consequences for the course of the action). Battle with the dragon and victory (H^1-I^1). Deliverance of the sister and the brothers (K^4). Return (↓).

$$\beta^1\gamma^2\zeta^1\eta^3\delta^2\theta^3A^1\left\{\frac{C\uparrow[D^1E^1 \text{ neg.}]^3[D^1E^1 \text{ neg.}]^3F \text{ contr}}{B^4C\uparrow[D^1E^1 \text{ pos.}]^3[D^1E^1 \text{ pos.}]^3}\right\}H^1\text{-}I^1K^4\downarrow$$

5. Analysis of a double-move tale. First move, of the class H-I, type: kidnapping of a person; second move, of the class M-N, type: seizure of booty, along with casting into a chasm.

139. I. A childless tsar, the marvelous birth of three sons and three steeds. The brothers leave home (↑), encounter the White Plainsman in a tent, fight (D^9). Two brothers are vanquished and thrown under a bed, the third is victorious (E^9). "Don't kill me"; he is accepted as a younger brother (i.e., helper [F^9]). Further along the journey they fight with the inhabitant of a forest hut (D^9E^9) who runs away. The entry into another kingdom is found by following his tracks (G^6). Sučénko lets himself down into it by a rope (G^5). "He remembered about the three princesses who were abducted into the other world by three dragons. 'I'll go to look for them.'" (A^1B^1C↑. Recollection employed not particularly well as the connective incident.) Three battles (H^1-I^1). Liberation (K^4). Transference of a ring (J^2); the third maiden is Súčenko's bride (w^1). Return (↓).

II. The brothers and the Plainsman abduct the maidens, cast down Sučénko ($*A^1$). Quest (C↑). Skirmish with an old man; Sučénko obtains the Water of Strength and a steed ($D^9E^9F_7{}^1$). Flight (G^1). Unrecognized arrival, service with a goldsmith (°). Claims of false heroes (L). The princesses demand rings (M). Iván sends the rings that had been received (N). The princesses still do not recognize the hero (Q neg.). He crawls through the ears of a horse (T^1), tears the roof off the house (X—provoked by the fact that the hero is not recognized). All are done three times. After the third time Sučénko swoops down upon the Plainsman and throws him to the ground from flight (U). The bride recognizes her betrothed (Q). Triple wedding (W*). See the scheme on page 139. In the tearing off of the roof one may observe a rudimentary form of a special function: the hero gives notice of himself. This function is not encountered in a pure aspect in our material. One of its forms is the throwing of a ring into a goblet, which is followed by recognition.

6. Analysis of a complicated five-move tale with the moves interwoven. The first move is of the class M-N, of the type: quest for a bride; the second move, without H-I or M-N, is of the type: mutilation; the third move, of the same class, is of the type: the taking away of the helper; the fourth is of the same class, and of the type: quest for brides; the fifth move, of the same class, is of the type: vampirism.

198. I. A tsar, his queen, their son (α). The parents place their son in the charge of the mentor Katóma (the future helper [F^1]); they die (β^2). The son desires to get married (a^1). Katóma shows some portraits to Iván (§), under one of which is the inscription: "If anyone shall pose her a riddle, him will she wed," †(task transferred to the connective incident.) Departure from home (C↑). The riddle is thought up en route by Katóma (solution beforehand [*N]). Katóma also accomplishes two other tasks for Iván (M-N). Wedding (W*).

II. After the marriage ceremony, the princess squeezes Iván's hand, recognizes his weakness, and guesses about Katóma's help (§). They go off to have a good time (β^3, absentation). The princess "subdues" Iván (η^3), he gives in to her caresses (θ^3). She orders Katóma's arms and legs chopped off (A^6, mutilation) and that he be thrown into the forest.††

† " 'Koli kto zadast ej zagadku, za togo pojdet zamuž' " (p. 137). The quotation is incomplete; a significant element has been omitted. The inscription in the tale actually reads: "Koli kto zadast ej zagadku, a korolevna ne otgadaet, za togo pojdet ona zamuž; a č'ju zagadku otgadaet, s togo golova doloj" (A. N. Afanás'ev, *Narodnye russkie skazki,* II [Goslitizdat, 1938], p. 127). ("If anyone shall pose her a riddle, and the queen does not solve it, him will she wed; but whose riddle she solves, off with his head.") [L.A.W.]

†† "Ona velit Katome otrubit' ruki i nogi . . . i vybrosit' ego v les" (p. 137). Actually, only Katoma's legs are chopped off. He is then put on top of a high stump at the wayside and abandoned there. [L.A.W.]

III. Iván's helper is taken away by force (A^{11}); he himself must pasture cows.

IV. (The tale follows Katóma). Legless Katóma meets a blind man (F_9^6, appearance of a helper and a proposal of services. Katóma is the hero of the given move.). They settle in the forest, contemplate the kidnapping of a merchant's daughter (a^1); they set out ($C\uparrow$); the blind man carries the legless one (G^2); they kidnap the merchant's daughter (K^1); they return ($\downarrow$). They are pursued and save themselves by running away (Pr^1-Rs^1).

V. A witch sucks the breasts of a maiden at night (A^{18}, vampirism). They plan how to save her (C). Skirmish with the witch (D^9-E^9). The maiden is saved (K^4).

II. (Development.) The witch shows them a healing well (F^2). They are cured by its water (K^5, liquidation of harm by application of a magical agent: Katóma gets back his arms and legs, and the blind man—his eyes.)

IV. (End.) The blind man marries the girl (W*).

III. (Development.) The heroes set out to rescue the prince ($C\uparrow$). Katóma presents his services anew to Iván (F^9); they free him from humiliating service (K^4). The peaceful continuation of Iván's and the princess' married life (w^2).

7. Analysis of a multi-move tale. The first move is of the class without H-I or M-N, and of the type: expulsion and substitution; the second move is the combination of H-I and M-N in one move, etc.

123. I. A king, his son (α). The king catches a forest spirit who begs the king's son to set him free (request of a prisoner, with preliminary capture [*D^4]). The prince lets him go (E^4, fulfillment). The forest spirit promises his aid (F^9). The prince is expelled (A^9), is given a manservant (appearance of the villain). They walk ($\uparrow$); en route the servant deceives the prince (η^3-θ^3), takes away his clothing and passes himself off as the king's son (A^{12}). The prince and the servant arrive unrecognized in another kingdom, the prince disguised as a cook (°). (We

omit an insignificant episode bearing no relation to the thread of the story.)

II. The forest spirit appears; his daughters give the prince a tablecloth, a looking-glass and a little flute (F^1). The princess "notices" the prince (not a function, nor a recognition, but a preparation for it). A dragon demands the princess (A^{16}). A call for aid (B^1). Departure of the prince and the man-servant ($C\uparrow$). The forest spirit appears, makes a gift of strength, a steed, and a sword (F_7^1). Battle with the dragon (H^1-I^1). The princess is saved (K^4). Return ($\downarrow$). The princess kisses the prince before the eyes of everyone (a rudiment of branding [J]). The servant demands the princess (L). The princess feigns illness, requires medicine (task).

III.–IV. Demand for medicine provokes a new move, i.e., we have an instance of a double significance. The princess needs medicine (α^6B^2). The prince and the man-servant set out in a boat ($C\uparrow$). IV. The servant drowns† the prince (A^{14}). The looking-glass gives a sign of alarm (B^4); the princess sets out to save him ($C\uparrow$). The forest spirit gives her a net (F^1). She drags the prince out (resuscitation K^9),† returns ($\downarrow$), tells all (exposure and recognition). The servant is shot (punishment). Wedding (W*).

8. Example of analysis of a tale with two heroes.

155. I. A soldier's wife, the marvelous birth of two sons, etc. (α). They desire to have horses (α^2), bid farewell (B^3), set out ($C\uparrow$). An old man interrogates them (D^2E^2), gives the horses (F^1). Up to that point two horses bought at the market had proved worthless (trebling).

II. The same; sabres are obtained.

III. The brothers leave home ($\uparrow$), take leave of each other by a post, transference of a kerchief ($<\gamma$). Fate of the first brother: he rides (G^2), arrives in a foreign land, marries a princess (W*). In the saddle he finds a vial con-

† The tale itself seems to imply that the princess rescues Iván before he has actually drowned. In any case, nothing is said about reviving him: the princess simply drags him out and takes him with her; at home she tells her father the whole story, and a feast, wedding, etc. follow. [L.A.W.]

taining the Water of Life and Healing (F^5, already relates to one of the following moves).

IV. The second brother learns of a dragon tormenting a princess ($A^{18}B^4$), C↑ follows, then three fights, a bandaged wound after the third. ($H^1J^1I^1$), liberation of the princess (K^1). The tsar dispatches a water-carrier to gather the bones of the princess (appearance of the false hero). He pretends to be the victor (L). After the third fight the hero enters the palace (§); he is recognized by his bandaged wound (Q); the false hero is exposed (Ex.) Punishment, wedding (UW*).

III. (Continuation.) The other brother goes hunting (absentation of the hero [β^3]). A beautiful girl begins to entice him (deception of the villain [η^3]). He submits (θ^3), she turns into a lioness and devours him. [A^{14}] murder. At the same time it serves as pursuit for the previous move. The lioness is the sister of the dragon.) The kerchief gives a signal of misfortune (B^4). The brother sets out (C↑). He rides on horseback (G^2). The lioness' deception; the hero does not give in (η^3-θ^3 neg.). He kills the she-dragon (I^5). She vomits forth the brother; he revives him (K^9). They pardon the lioness (U neg.).† Return of both brothers (↓). Subsequently the lioness destroys them both (A=X).

$$\text{I.-II.}\quad \alpha^2B^3C\uparrow D^2E^2F^1=K\downarrow$$

$$\left.\begin{array}{ll}\text{III.} & \uparrow<\gamma G^2W^*F^5\ldots A^{14}B^4C\uparrow G^2I^5K^9U\text{-}\\ \text{IV.} & \quad\ldots A^{18}B^4C\uparrow H^1J^1I^1K^1LQExUW^*\end{array}\right\}\downarrow X$$

† "Obman l'vicy, geroj ne poddaetsja [η^3—$\theta^3_{neg.}$]. On ubivaet zmeixu [I^5]. Ona otrygivaet brata, on ego oživljaet [K^9]. L'vicu proščajut [U_{neg}]. . ." (p. 139). The apparent paradox of a dead creature spitting up her victim and later being pardoned is due to an error of analysis, and may be resolved by reference to the tale itself. The she-dragon, the lioness, and the beautiful girl are one and the same creature, of course, and the first Iván only *threatens* to kill her, he does not actually do so (cf. the footnote on p. 127). After reviving his brother, the first Ivan wants to chop off the lioness' head, but she turns back into a beautiful girl and beseeches him to forgive her. He succumbs to her entreaties and lets her go. [L.A.W.]

APPENDIX III

SCHEMES AND COMMENTARY † ††

† An explanatory comment on the schemes and their symbolization is given by the author in footnote 4, Chapter IX. [L.A.W.]

†† The original transcriptions (which employ different symbols than those used in this translation) contain a number of misprints and other inconsistencies, evident in many cases by a lack of correspondence between the scheme of a tale presented here, and the symbolization employed in the commentary or analysis of the same tale elsewhere (e.g. in Appendix II, and at the end of this appendix). Wherever such comparative material existed, the symbolization overall was made consistent, insofar as possible. However, for those schemes which could not be correlated elsewhere in this text, no significant changes were made; they are transcribed essentially as presented. [L.A.W.]

Tale (new No.)	Move	D	E	F		A	B	C		↑	D	E	F	G		
93	I					A^{xvii}	B^3			↑	d^7	E_-^7	F_-			
	II					α^6	B^3		F^1	↑	d^7	E_+^7	F_+^1			
	III[1]					A^{xvii}				↑						
95	I					A^9	B^5				D^1	E^1	f^1			
	II					$[\alpha^6]$	B_2^5	C		↑	D^1	E_-^1	F_-			
98	I					A^9	B^5			↑ {	D^7	E^7	f^9	}		
											D^1	E^1	f^1			
	II					α^6	B_2^5	C		↑ {	D^7	E_-^7	F_-^9	}		
											D^1	E_-^1	F_-			
100						A^{ii}					D^3	E^3	F^{vi}			
101	II					A_{12}^{11}	B^7	C		↑					K^8	
104	I			F^1		α^6	B^2	C		↑	D^1	E^1	F^1			
												{	F^3			
	II					$[\alpha^1]$							F^4			
105	I					A^3	B^4	C	F_4^3	↑						
	II	D^8	E^8	F^8[2]		α^1		C		↑	D^8	E^8	F^8			
106	I, II					A^1	B^4	C		↑						
	III					A^1	B^4			↑	D^8	E^8				
108						A^1				↑	D^8	E^8				
113						A^1		C		↑ {	D^1	E_-^1	F_-	} G^4		
											d^7	E^7	F^9			
114						A^{xvi}			{		d^7	E^7	F_3^2			
										↑	D^8	E^8	F^8			
115	I					A^6				↑		E^7	F^2			
	II					A^{18}	B^4	C			D^1	E^1	F^1			

1 Elements H-I (struggle) and Pr-Rs (pursuit) are transposed.

2 F^1? Cf. the tale itself. [L.A.W.]

3 $D^1E^1F^9$ is inverted between Pr–Rs.

L	H M	J	I N		K	↓	Pr	Rs		L	Q	Ex	T		U	W*
	Pr^1		Rs^2				H^4	I^4								w*
						↓ ↓										
						↓ ↓										
	M		N													W*
	M		N									Ex			U	w^2
	  M		 *N *N N	}		↓									U	W**
					K^7	↓ ↓	 Pr^1	 Rs^2								
					K^1	↓ ↓										
						↓	Pr^7 { Pr^7 {	Rs^{10} Rs^1	}							
					K^1	↓	Pr^1	Rs^{43}								
						 ↓	Pr Pr^1	Rs^4 Rs^2	}0		Q					W*
			I^6		K^5											W*

Tale (new No.)	Move	D	E	F		A	B	C		↑	D	E	F	G		0
125	I	D^4	E^4	F^9		A^9				↑						0
	II			F_7^1		A^{16}		C		↑						
126	I					A^3	B^2	C		↑						
	II	*D^4	E^4	F^9		A^{19}	B^3	C					F^1			
127						A^6			0				F_4^3			
128	I					α^1	B^2	C		↑	D^1	E^1	F^5	G^5		
	II				J^2	*A^1		C		↑			F^1	G^1		
131						A^1	B^1	C		↑						
132	I					A^5	B^1	C		↑						
	II					[α^6]		C	F^3	↑	D^1	E^1	{ F^5 F_7^1	G^5 G^2 }		
	III					*A^1		C		↑	d^7	E^7	F^9	G^1		0
133	I					A^1		C		↑	D^1	E_{-}^1	F_{-}			
	II						B^4	C		↑	D^1	E^1				
135						A^4		C					F^3			
136	I					α^6	B^1	C			D^2	E^2				
	II					A^1	B^2	C								
	III					A^1		C								
137	I	↑D^1	E^1	F^5		A^{19}		C								
	II					α^1	B^2	C	F_2^1	↑		[K^{10}]	F_9^6			
138	I					α^3	B^1	C		↑	D^2	E^2	F_4^2	G^2		
	II					A^2		C		↑	D^1	E^2	F_9^3	G^1		
	III					α^1		C		↑						
139	I	↑D^9	E^9	F^9	G_5^6	A^1	B^1	C		↑						
	II					*A^1		C		↑	D^9	E^9	F_7^1	G^1		0

L	H M	J	I N		K	↓	Pr	Rs		L	Q	Ex	T		U	W
	H^1	J^1	I^1		K^4	↓	Pr	Rs	}	L	Q	Ex			U	W*
	H^1	J^1	I^1	↓	K^7 K^3	↓			T^2		Q					W*
					K^3	T^2	Pr^6	Rs^6			Q	Ex			U	W*
					K^1											W^1 W*
	H^1		I^1		K^4	↓										W^0
	M		I^5 N		K_{-}^7	↓ ↓					Q	Ex			U	W*
	H^1		I^1		K^4	↓										
	H^1		I^1		K^4	↓ {	Pr^4 Pr^1	Rs^7 Rs^5	}							
	H^1		I^1		KF^2 KF^5 K^1	↓ {	Pr^4 Pr^2	Rs^7 Rs^5	}							
{	H^1 M M		I^1 N N		K^4	↓ ↓	Pr^4	Rs^7							U	W*
. . .	H^1 . III M	. . .	I^1 . . . N	. . .	K^4 K^4 K^1	↓ { ↓ ↓	Pr^4 Pr^4	Rs^7 Rs^7								W*
	H^1 M		I^1 N		K^4						Q_{-}		T^1	J^2 X		W^1↓ UQW*

Tale (new No.)	Move	D	E	F		A	B	C		↑	D	E	F	G		
140						A^1	B^1	C		↑	D^9	E^9		G^6	F^7	
141	I					A^9			F^1	↑ {	D^9	E^9	F_9^6 F^9	} G^6	F^2	
	II					*A^1		C		↑			F^6	G^5		
143	I					A^3		C	F^1	↑						
	II					A^9				↑			F_9^6			
144						[a^1]	M	C		↑			$F^2F_9^6$	G^1		
145						a^1	B^2	C		↑			F^3	G^1		
148						A^1	B_2^4	C		↑						
149						A^{17}	B^4	C		↑						
150	I	D	E		X	a^6	B^2	C		↑						
	II					a^5	B^2	C		↑						
151						a^5	B^4	C		↑						
152						A^9				↑						
153						A^{18}		C		↑			F^1			
154		↑D	E^7	F^9_	G^1T^4	A^{18}		C		↑			F^1			
155	I-II					a^2	B^3	C		↑	D^2	E^2	F^1			
	III	↑<Y G^2 W* F^5. . .				A^{14}	B^4	C		↑				G^2		
	IV				. . .	A^{18}	B^4	C		↑						
156	I					A^1	B^3	C		↑ {	D^2 D^1	E^2 E^1	F^2 F^6	G^2 G^5	}	
	II					a^4	B^4	C		↑	*D^4	E^4	F_9^6	G^5		
	III			F^2		*A^7		C		↑				G^1		o
159	I					A^1		C		↑	· · ·	· ·	·II·	· · ·	· · ·	· ·
	II				W*	A^1		C		↑			F^9			
	III					A_1^{14}	} B^4	C		↑						
								C		↑						

L	H M	J	I N		K	↓	Pr	Rs		L	Q	Ex	T		U	W*
			I^5		K^4	↓										W*
			I^5		K^4 K^4	↓									U	W*
	H^1 H^1		I^1 I^1		K^7 K^1	↓ ↓										W*
	M		N										T^3			W*
					K^2	↓										
	H^1		I^1		K^4	↓										W_*
	H^2	{	I^2 I_2^6		K^4	↓										w°
	H^2		I^2		K^7 K^1	↓ ↓	Rs	Pr							U	w°
	H^2		I^2		K^1	↓										
	H^2		I^2		K^1	↓										
	H^3		I^3	X											Uw°↓X	
	H^3		I^3		K^4											W*
	H^1	J^1	I^5[1] I^1		K K^9[1] K^1	↓				L	Q	Ex		U_ U	W*	}↓X
L	M		N		K^4 K^2	↓									U {U	w^1 W* W*}
. . . . .	II	. . .	. . .	. . .	K^4 K^4 K^9 K^4	 ↓ ↓	 Pr^1 Pr^1	 Rs^1 Rs^1[2]								

1 Cf. p. 58, footnote. [L.A.W.]

2 H^1-I^1 follows. Move IV is inserted between K^4 and ↓.

Tale (new No.)	Move	D	E	F		A	B	C		↑	D	E	F	G		o
159	IV					α^2		C	F^1	↑	{ *D D^1	E E^1	F^9 F^8	}		
161	I					A^{19}	B^2	C		↑						
	II					α^1		C		↑			F^1	G^3		
	III					α^1		C		↑	D^9	E^9	{ F^4	G^6 G^5 }		
	IV					α^1		C		↑				G^2		
162		D^6	E^6	F^1		A^{11}	. . . . .	. . . . .	. . . . .	. . . . .	· ‖ ·	. . . . .	. . . . .	. . . . .	. . . . .	. . . . .
						A^1	B^3	C		↑						
163					{	α^1	F_6^9	C		↑				G^3		
164	I					A^5		C		↑						
	II				{	[α^1]	F^9	C		↑			T^4 T^4	G^3		
166	I	*D^4	E^4	F^9		A^8				↑				G^1		
	II					A^{10}								G^2		
167	I					α^5					D	E	F^9			
	II				W*	A^{10}	B^3	C		↑				G^2		
	III					α^1	B^3	C								

L	H M	J	I N		K	↓	Pr	Rs		L	Q	Ex	T		U	W
					KF^8	↓	Pr^1	Rs^2								
	H^1		I^1		K^4	↓										
	H^1		I^1		KF^9											
			I^5		K^4											
	H^1		I^1													W*
	H^1		I^1		K^8	} ↓										W*
	H^1		I^1		K^4											
													T^4			W*↓ }
			I^5													W*
					K^7	↓										
																W*↓ }
			I^5													W *
																W*
													T^2	Q		
					K^6								T · ·	· ·	U	W*
	M		N													W*↓

We have written out one half of our material. The question arises whether it is necessary to write out the rest. The reader will believe us if we say that new material adds nothing, and the investigator will convince himself of this if he continues the analyses.

Notes on Individual Schemes

93. This tale is quite complicated. We shall give a complete analysis of it.

I. A tsar, his queen, their son (α). The groom predicts (§) the birth of a sister who shall be a terrible witch; she shall devour her father and mother and all people under their command (A^{xvii}, threat of cannibalism through relatives). Iván asks permission to go out for a walk; he is allowed to do so (B^3); he flees (↑), encounters two old seamstresses: "When we use up the chest full of needles and the chest full of thread, death will come immediately" (d^7, helpless situation without a request). The hero can do nothing for them (E^7 neg.). They give him nothing (F neg.). The same occurs with Oak-Turner who is uprooting the last oak trees, and with Mountain-Turner who is overturning the last mountains. Iván comes to the Sun's sister.

II. Iván is sad (§). The Sun's sister interrogates him three times $(\varepsilon^8\text{-}\zeta^8)^{2+1}$. He longs to go home ($\alpha^6$); she releases him ($B^3$), gives him a brush, a comb, and two rejuvenating apples (F^1). He leaves (↑). A meeting again with Mountain-Turner, Oak-Turner, and the seamstresses. He gives them the brush, the comb, and the apples (the brush = new mountains, a new life for Mountain-Turner; the comb = new oak trees; the apples = rejuvenation for the old women [E^7, a service rendered]). The old women present him with a scarf (F^1). Iván arrives home.

III. The sister says, "Play a little on the gusla" (η^1, deceitful persuasion). Mice forewarn (§) that she went out to sharpen her teeth (A^{xvii}). Iván does not give in to the deception (θ^3 neg.), and flees (↑). The witch is catching up (Pr^1, pursuit). Oak-Turner piles up oak trees, Mountain-Turner sets down mountains, the scarf turns into a lake (Rs^2, rescue by obstacle). He arrives at the "Sister's." The she-dragon † says, "Let Prince Iván get on the

† Cf. the footnote on p. 66 in regard to the term *zmeixa* (she-dragon) used here. [L.A.W.]

scales to see who will outweigh whom" (H^4). The scales give the superiority to Iván (I^4). He remains forever with the Sun's sister (w*, a rudimentary form of marriage).

94. "Vólga and Vazúza," a tale of a different class.

97. The same construction as that of tale No. 95. The second move is missing.

99. The same as No. 98.

101. I=100 I.

102. =95.

104. II. A more complicated case.

II. A girl, a miraculous doll (α). She goes to town, settles in an old woman's house (o, unrecognized arrival). The old woman buys her some flax (F^4), from which she spins unusually fine yarn (see below). In one night the doll makes a loom for her (F^8). She weaves unusually fine linen (see below). The old woman takes the linen to the tsar (§). He orders that shirts be sewn by the one who has spun and woven the linen (task). The girl sews the shirts (solution). The tsar sends for the girl (§), wedding and coronation of Vasilísa (W^*_*). This case is not quite clear at first glance. It is obvious, however, that the spinning, weaving, and sewing is a trebling of one element. Sewing is the solution of the task posed by the tsar. That the commission to sew shirts is really a difficult task is seen in the fact that no one undertakes to sew them, and then the tsar announces through the old woman, "You knew how to spin and weave such linen; know also how to sew shirts from it." Consequently, spinning and weaving are also the solutions of tasks, while the task itself is omitted. This is a case of preliminary solution (*N). First comes the solution, and then the task. This is evident from the girl's words: "I knew that this work would not bypass my hands." She *foresees* the task. The purchase of the flax and the manufacture of the loom are related to the transference of magical agents. It is true that nothing magical exists in the flax, but it is a means for fulfillment of the task. The loom, to a greater extent, bears a magical character. The third task is resolved without the preliminary receipt of any sort of means, but one may suppose that the transference of some sort of (very thin, etc.) needle was omitted here. Further, we see that there appears to be no complication (*zavjázka*) in this move. But the entire action stems from the situation that the tsar has no wife. It is not referred to in words, but Vasilísa's actions are all dictated by this situation. She possesses the gift of foresight, and the purchase of flax, etc., is provoked by a longing for her royal betrothed. If this element is designated by sign α^1, the scheme will give:

$$[\alpha^1]\left\{\begin{matrix} F^3\text{-}{*}N \\ F^4\text{-}{*}N \\ M\text{-}N \end{matrix}\right\} W^{*}_{*}$$

105. II. D^8-E^8 is conditionally designated as a struggle with a mare. The taming of a horse does not usually amount to a function (see Appendix I, Table V, No. 88). It is made use of here as D, preparing F (the transference of the colt helpers).

114. I. A brother calls his sister to the feather bed. Conditionally designated as Pr, without relation to the type. The action of dolls, by whose singing the girl sinks into the ground, is conditionally designated Rs^4 (rescue by concealment).

123. This tale was analyzed earlier. It is not included in the scheme, since inclusion of tales containing H-I and M-N in one move creates a motley in which it is difficult to make headway at first glance.

125. Two insignificant episodes are not included in the scheme; elements Pr-Rs are highly confused, belonging to no type.

127. A more complicated instance.

A merchant's daughter is the bride of the tsar. (α, expanded epically). She travels to the king (β^3). A servant girl puts the bride to sleep (η^2-θ^2), digs out her eyes (A^6); unrecognized arrival, the girl at a herdsman's (°). The bride asks the herdsman to buy her some silk and some velvet, she embroiders a miraculous crown (F_4^3), wins back her eyes with the help of the crown (K^8). During the night the girl suddenly awakens in a palace (T^2). The tsar sees the palace, invites the girl to be his guest (§). The servant girl orders the gendarmes to hack her to death (Pr^6, fulfillment assimilated with A^{13}; her heart is ordered to be presented). The old man buries the remains, from which a garden grows up (Rs^6, by means of transformation). The servant-queen orders the garden cut down (Pr^6). The garden turns to stone (Rs^6). A boy appears (ex machina) and wheedles the heart away from the queen with the help of bitter tears (K^8-Rs). The girl suddenly appears (the text is not quite clear, but in any case, K^9). Recognition (Q) follows along with exposure (Ex); the bride recounts everything. Punishment; wedding.

The last of three pursuits has assimilated with A^{13}-K^8.

136. The fourth move contains both H-I and M-N according to the scheme:

$$\alpha^1 C[H^1\text{-}I^1]^3 \begin{cases} \text{M-N W*} \\ \text{M-NUw}^2 \end{cases}$$

Here, α^1 has assimilated with A^{16}. The hero claims the princess with a threat, as a dragon usually does.

150. A more complicated case which we quote in its entirety.

I. A peasant and his three sons (α). The eldest goes off to a merchant's to serve as a hired man, but he cannot endure it and returns. This is purely a motif of everyday life and may be examined as a deformation of service at a witch's. Compare the service of Truth at a merchant's, etc. We designate it D-E without designating the type. The youngest son saves himself by cleverness (E, the rooster is lulled asleep). The hired man demonstrates his strength on a bull (X). The merchant fears the hired man (mot.). A cow of his allegedly gets lost, (a^6); he dispatches the hired man (B^2), who sets out (C↑); he catches a bear (K^7), and returns (↓).

II. The merchant is all the more afraid (mot.), sends the hired man for money supposedly given to devils (a^5B^2); he sets out (C↑). Three contests with the devils (H^2-I^2). Much money is obtained (K^1, with details), return (↓). The merchant and his wife run away from the hired man. The hired man follows them in a shrewd manner. (Humorous inversion: the villain runs away instead of the hero; the hero pursues [Rs-Pr]). The hired man kills the merchant (U), takes his property for himself (w°).

This tale, while generally retaining the structure of fairy tales, cannot be explained exhaustively without drawing upon the material of tales of other classes.

The remaining cases present no special difficulties, although a great deal may be said about separate details.

APPENDIX IV

LIST OF ABBREVIATIONS †

Preparatory section

α initial situation
β^1 absentation (departure) of elders
β^2 death of parents
β^3 absentation (departure) of younger people
γ^1 interdiction
γ^2 order or command
δ^1 interdiction violated
δ^2 order or command carried out
ε^1 reconnaissance by the villain to obtain information about the hero
ε^2 reconnaissance by the hero to obtain information about the villain
ε^3 reconnaissance by other persons
ζ^1 the villain receives information about the hero
ζ^2 the hero receives information about the villain
ζ^3 information received by other means
η^1 deceitful persuasions of the villain
η^2 application of magical agents by the villain
η^3 other forms of deception or coercion
θ^1 the hero reacts to the persuasions of a villian
θ^2 the hero mechanically falls victim to the influence of a magical agent
θ^3 the hero gives in or reacts mechanically to the deceit of the villain
λ preliminary misfortune caused by a deceitful agreement

A *Villainy*

† The original list has been somewhat modified and enlarged to achieve a closer and fuller correspondence with the symbols and definitions employed in the text itself. [L.A.W.]

*A villainy accompanied by casting into a chasm, etc. (in the second move)

A^{1} kidnapping of a person

A^{2} seizure of a magical agent or helper

A^{ii} the forcible seizure of a magical helper

A^{3} the ruining of crops

A^{4} theft of daylight

A^{5} plundering in various forms

A^{6} maiming, mutilation

A^{7} evocation of disappearance

A^{vii} the bride is forgotten (tale No. 219)

A^{8} demand for delivery or enticement, abduction

A^{9} expulsion

A^{10} casting into the sea

A^{11} the casting of a spell; a transformation

A^{12} false substitution

A^{13} an order to kill

A^{14} murder

A^{15} imprisonment, detention

A^{16} the threat of forced matrimony

A^{xvi} the threat of forced matrimony between relatives

A^{17} the threat of cannibalism

A^{xvii} the threat of cannibalism among relatives

A^{18} tormenting at night (vampirism)

A^{19} declaration of war

a *Lack, Insufficiency*

a^{1} lack of a bride, of an individual

a^{2} lack of a helper or magical agent

a^{3} lack of wondrous objects

a^{4} lack of the egg of death (of love)

a^{5} lack of money or the means of existence

a^{6} lacks in other forms

B *Mediation, the connective incident*

B^{1} call for help

B^{2} dispatch

B^{3} release; departure

B^{4} announcement of misfortune in various forms

B^{5} transportation of banished hero

B^{6} condemned hero released, spared

B^7 lament or plaintive song

C *Consent to counteraction*

↑ *Departure, dispatch of the hero from home*

D *The first function of the donor*

D^1 test of the hero

D^2 greeting, interrogation

D^3 request for a favor after death

D^4 entreaty of a prisoner for freedom

$*D^4$ entreaty of a prisoner for freedom, with preliminary imprisonment

D^5 request for mercy

D^6 request for division

d^6 argument without an expressed request for division

D^7 other requests

$*D^7$ other requests, with preliminary helpless situation of the person making the request

d^7 helpless situation of the donor without a stated request; the possibility of rendering service

D^8 attempt to destroy

D^9 combat with a hostile donor

D^{10} the offer of a magical agent as an exchange

E *Reaction of the hero* (positive or negative)

E^1 sustained ordeal

E^2 friendly response

E^3 favor to a dead person

E^4 freeing of a captive

E^5 mercy to a suppliant

E^6 separation of disputants

E^{vi} deception of disputants

E^7 performance of some other service; fulfillment of a request; pious deeds

E^8 attempt at destruction averted

E^9 victory in combat

E^{10} deception in an exchange

F *The acquisition, receipt of a magical agent*

F^1 the agent is transferred

f^1	the gift is of a material nature
F neg (F–)	the agent is not transferred
F contr. (F=)	hero's negative reaction provokes cruel retribution
F^2	the agent is pointed out
F^3	the agent is prepared
F^4	the agent is sold, purchased
F_4^3	the agent is made on order
F^5	the agent is found
F^6	the agent appears of its own accord
F^{vi}	the agent appears from out of the earth
F_9^6	meeting with a helper who offers his services
F^7	the agent is drunk or eaten
F^8	the agent is seized
F^9	the agent offers its services, places itself at someone's disposal.
f^9	the agent indicates it will appear of its own accord in some time of need
G	*Transference to a designated place; guidance*
G^1	the hero flies through the air
G^2	the hero rides, is carried
G^3	the hero is led
G^4	the route is shown to the hero
G^5	the hero makes use of stationary means of communication
G^6	a bloody trail shows the way
H	*The hero struggles with the villain*
H^1	fight in an open field
H^2	a contest, competition
H^3	a game of cards
H^4	weighing
I	*Victory over the villain*
I^1	victory in open battle
$*I^1$	victory by one hero while the other(s) hide
I^2	victory or superiority in a contest
I^3	winning at cards
I^4	superiority in weighing
I^5	killing of the villain without a fight
I^6	expulsion of the villain

J *Branding or marking the hero*
J^1 application of a mark to the body
J^2 the transference of a ring or towel

K *The liquidation of misfortune or lack*
K^1 direct acquisition through the application of force or cunning
K^1 the same, with one person compelling another to accomplish the acquisition in question
K^2 acquisition accomplished by several helpers at once
K^3 acquisition achieved with the help of an enticement or decoys
K^4 liquidation of misfortune as the direct result of previous actions
K^5 misfortune is done away with instantly through the use of a magical agent
K^6 poverty is done away with through the use of a magical agent
K^7 object of search is captured
K^8 breaking of a spell
K^9 resuscitation
K^{ix} the same, with the preliminary obtaining of the Water of Life
K^{10} release from captivity
KF liquidation in form F, that is:
KF^1 the object of a search is transferred;
KF^2 the object of a search is pointed out, etc.

↓ *Return of the hero*

Pr *Pursuit of the hero*
Pr^1 flight through the air
Pr^2 demand for the guilty person
Pr^3 pursuit, accompanied by a series of transformations into animals
Pr^4 pursuit, with transformations into enticing objects
Pr^5 attempt to devour the hero
Pr^6 attempt to destroy the hero
Pr^7 attempt to gnaw through a tree

Rs	*Rescue of the hero*
Rs^1	he is carried through the air or runs quickly
Rs^2	he throws comb, etc., in the path of his pursuers
Rs^3	fleeing, with transformation into a church, etc.
Rs^4	fleeing, with concealment of the escapee
Rs^5	concealment of the escapee by blacksmiths
Rs^6	series of transformations into animals, plants and stones
Rs^7	warding off of the temptation of enticing objects
Rs^8	rescue or salvation from being devoured
Rs^9	rescue or salvation from being destroyed
Rs^{10}	leap to another tree
o	*Unrecognized arrival*
L	*Claims of a false hero*
M	*Difficult task*
N	*Solution (resolution) of a task*
*N	solution before a deadline
Q	*Recognition of the hero*
Ex	*Exposure of the false hero*
T	*Transfiguration*
T^1	new physical appearance
T^2	the building of a palace
T^3	new garments
T^4	humorous and rationalized forms
U	*Punishment of the false hero or villain*
U neg.	false hero or villain pardoned
W^{*}_{*}	*Wedding and accession to the throne*
W^{*}	wedding
W_{*}	accession to the throne
w^{*}	rudimentary form of marriage (tale no. 93)
w^1	promised marriage
w^2	resumed marriage
w°	monetary reward and other forms of material gain at the dénouement
X	*Unclear or alien forms*

<	*Leave-taking at a road marker*
Y	*Transmission of a signaling device*
mot.	*Motivations*
pos. or +	*Positive result for a function*
neg. or –	*Negative result for a function*
§	*Connectives*
⁝	*Connectives trebled*

APPENDIX V

COMPARATIVE CHART OF TALE NUMBERS

A comparative list of the newer and older numerical designations of tales appearing in the collection *Narodnye russkie skazki* by Afánas'ev, and cited in this work.

NEW NUMBER (Number of the tale in the 5th [1936–1940] and 6th [1957] editions.)	OLD NUMBER (Number of the tale in the 2nd, 3rd, and 4th editions.)	NEW NUMBER (Number of the tale in the 5th [1936–1940] and 6th [1957] editions.)	OLD NUMBER (Number of the tale in the 2nd, 3rd, and 4th editions.)
53	23a	125	68
93	50	126	69
94	51	127	70
95	52a	128	71a
97	53	130	71c
98	54	131	72
99	55	132	73
100	56	133	74a
101	57	135	75
102	58a	136	76
104	59	137	77
105	60	138	78
106	61a	139	79
108	62a	140	80
113	64	141	81a
114	65	143	82
115	66a	144	83
123	67a	145	84a

NEW NUMBER (Number of the tale in the 5th [1936–1940] and 6th [1957] editions.)	OLD NUMBER (Number of the tale in the 2nd, 3rd, and 4th editions.)	NEW NUMBER (Number of the tale in the 5th [1936–1940] and 6th [1957] editions.)	OLD NUMBER (Number of the tale in the 2nd, 3rd, and 4th editions.)
148	85	192	113a
149	86	195	114a
150	87	196	114b
151	88	197	115
152	89	198	116a
153	90	201	117
154	91	202	118a
155	92	204	118c
156	93a	208	120a
159	94	209	120b
160	95	210	121a
161	96	212	122a
162	97	216	123
163	98	219	125a
164	99	227	126a
165	100a	230	127a
166	100b	232	128a
167	101	234	129a
168	102	236	130a
169	103a	238	131
170	103b	239	132
171	104a	240	133
179	105a	241	134
180	105b	242	135
182	106a	243	136
185	107	244	137a
186	108	247	138
187	109	248	139
189	111	249	140a
190	112a	258	144

NEW NUMBER (Number of the tale in the 5th [1936–1940] and 6th [1957] editions.)	OLD NUMBER (Number of the tale in the 2nd, 3rd, and 4th editions.)	NEW NUMBER (Number of the tale in the 5th [1936–1940] and 6th [1957] editions.)	OLD NUMBER (Number of the tale in the 2nd, 3rd, and 4th editions.)
259	145	266	149
260	146a	267	150a
264	147	270	151
265	148		